SCRIPTURAL BAPTISM

ITS MODE & SUBJECTS AS OPPOSED TO
THE VIEWS OF THE ANABAPTISTS

T. WITHEROW

Published by Left of Brain Books

Copyright © 2021 Left of Brain Books

ISBN 978-1-396-31790-3

First Edition

All rights reserved. No part of this publication may be reproduced, distributed, or transmitted in any form or by any means, including photocopying, recording, or other electronic or mechanical methods, without the prior written permission of the publisher, except in the case of brief quotations embodied in critical reviews and certain other noncommercial uses permitted by copyright law. Left of Brain Books is a division of Left of Brain Onboarding Pty Ltd.

Table of Contents

INTRODUCTORY.	1
THE MODE OF BAPTISM.	3
I. Difficulties connected with Dipping.	3
II. Dipping not proved by the Scriptures.	5
III. The Scriptural Mode of Baptism.	14
IV. Conclusion.	17
THE SUBJECTS OF BAPTISM.	20
I. The Question in Debate.	20
II. Anabaptist Objections.	23
III. Evidence for Infant Baptism.	28
IV. The Apostolic Commission.	34
V. Additional Considerations.	38
VI. No proof on the Anabaptist side.	46
VII. The Parable of the City Park.	47
Conclusion.	55

To the Reader.

This little work is, under a new title, the substance of three Tracts which were published in 1859-60, during the Revival in Ulster. Everything of a local and personal nature has now been omitted; and a few other things also, which I could wish to have retained, but which brevity has induced me to sacrifice. The tract on MODE was very hurriedly got up, having been originally written in a single day, to meet an exigency of that time. It has been now rearranged, and, to some extent, re-written.

It is humbly hoped that, in its new form, this little Book on Baptism will be more worthy of general acceptance.

INTRODUCTORY.

SALVATION comes to us from God. His eternal purpose in regard to it is carried into execution by His Son and by His Spirit. The great work of the Son is to make atonement for sin by His death; the great work of the Spirit is to produce within us a new nature. From the one we receive our title to heaven, from the other our meetness for heaven. By faith in Christ we are justified; by the grace of the Spirit we are sanctified. The work of each is equally necessary to the eternal happiness of men. The same Bible that says, "He that hath not the Son of God hath not life," also expressly teaches that, "Except a man be born again, he cannot see the kingdom of God."

It is a striking evidence of God's care for the best interests of His people, that He has adopted means, under both Dispensations, for keeping prominently before the minds of men truths so indispensable to salvation. He has appointed in His Church ordinances to be symbols of the greatest facts in human redemption. The work of the Son was represented to God's people in ancient times by the Lamb of the Passover, which was an emblem of "Christ our Passover sacrificed for us:" but it is represented to us by the Lord's Supper, with regard to which it is testified that, "As often as ye eat this bread and drink this cup, ye do show the Lord's death till He come." The symbol of the Passover has now given way to the symbol of the Supper; but the great truth embodied in both ordinances—redemption by the blood of Christ—is always the same. In like manner, the work of the Spirit was of old shadowed forth in the rite of circumcision—the emblem of purification—a symbolical action that represented the sanctifying effects of grace upon the heart; but it is exhibited to us in the ordinance of Baptism, which is a symbolical action that figures forth the removal of sin. The symbol of circumcision has retired to make way for the symbol of baptism; but the great truth embodied in them both—the sanctification of the Holy Ghost—is ever the same. The two symbolic ordinances of the Gospel Dispensation thus serve an important end in the economy of grace. By visible emblems they speak great truths to the eye. The Supper presents the work of Christ; Baptism presents the work of the

Spirit. God says to us through the one, "Believe on the Lord Jesus Christ and thou shalt be saved;" but He says to us in the other, Wash you, make you clean; Turn you at my reproof; Behold I will pour out my Spirit unto you."

The ordinance of Baptism is a question on which great diversity of opinion prevails throughout the Church of God. It is generally agreed that the proper element to be used is water, and that the rite is to be administered in the name of the Trinity. Different opinions, however, are entertained in reference to other departments of the subject, any one of which would open up an interesting field for inquiry. Two of these topics it is our design to examine at present. We propose to discuss the *Mode of Baptism,* and the *Subjects of Baptism,* and to gather from the Word of God, as best we can, what it teaches on these matters.

THE MODE OF BAPTISM.

THE opinion held by Anabaptists on this subject is that, "Immersion, or dipping of the person in water, is necessary to the due administration of the ordinance;" that, in fact, dipping is so essential to baptism, that every person undipped is, in reality, unbaptised. This notion is simple and intelligible enough, but *is it true?*

I. Difficulties connected with Dipping.

The Anabaptist opinion implies, of course, that every instance of baptism mentioned in Scripture was a case of immersion. But the very statement of such a thing suggests to every intelligent man a host of difficulties, which, though not of themselves, perhaps, sufficient to disprove immersion, are strong enough to raise grave doubts whether it was practised by the Apostles of Christ, or made binding on future generations. Of these difficulties, the following are a specimen:—

1. We know from Acts ii. 41, that three thousand persons were, on the day of Pentecost, baptized at Jerusalem. The difficulty that strikes every mind that has acquaintance with the place is, Where was the water found to dip such a multitude? No river passes the city; the nearest lake is many miles away; the brook Cedron is the dry bed of a little stream which only flows in the winter months; only three wells are known to exist in or around the city, in two of which the water in summer—the time at which Pentecost always occurs—is more than sixty feet under ground, and the third is only a little stream trickling from a rock, and lost in the nearest garden: and during all the summer months the inhabitants depend on the rain water of the previous winter, carefully kept in cisterns for public accommodation, or in tanks under the houses, up out of which the water required for domestic purposes is drawn by a bucket and a wheel. In such circumstances, one cannot help asking, *Where were these three thousand people dipped?*

2. The numbers that came to John's baptism constitute another well-known difficulty. "Then went out to him Jerusalem, and all Judæa, and all the region round about Jordan, and were baptized of him in Jordan." Reckoning the population of the district at a million, which, by the best accounts, is too low a figure, and supposing that only one-third of these came out for baptism (and less could scarcely be supposed in accordance with the general terms employed), then it would have taken John three years and a half to have dipped one-third of the population, allowing him to baptize one person every two minutes, and to work ten hours a day! Yet John's ministry, as all agree, did not continue over six months; and it is not in evidence that he, like his Master, had any assistants in his work. If, in so short a time, John dipped Jerusalem and all the region round about Jordan, he must have lived in the water more than half his time. Against no form of baptism except immersion does this difficulty hold. One could, in the time specified, sprinkle a much greater multitude with ease. If one man dipped 300,000 in six months, would the Anabaptist kindly tell us *how it was done?*

3. Dipping in the presence of a multitude implies an exposure of the person, from which many, especially modest and delicate females, shrink, and often live undipped for years rather than encounter. Yet how strange it seems that at John's baptism no one seems to have felt surprised at the novel rite; none objected to it; none hesitated; none, so far as we know, lingered on year after year without being able to summon up courage to submit to the rite. Either human nature is very different now from what it was then, or else John's baptism was not dipping.

4. Immersion is a mode of baptism ill-suited to a universal religion. In a tropical climate, where water is scarce, a man might live half a lifetime without seeing as much water in one place as would be sufficient to dip a man; in a polar region, where for more than half the year ice and snow are everywhere around, dipping would be almost impossible; while, again, there are many constitutions so delicate and tender, that to them dipping would be death. Some are known to have had their health seriously impaired, and their lives endangered, by submitting to this form of the ordinance. On the contrary, there is no place where a human being dwells that the washing of water is not possible, and in no circumstances is it ever unsafe. We conclude, therefore,

that dipping is not the mode of baptism best adapted to a universal religion, such as Christianity was designed to be.

These difficulties may not be strong enough to disprove immersion, and must, of course, give way, if clear and convincing evidence be forthcoming on its behalf; but, taken together, they are serious enough to raise doubts about the matter, and to make us look very sharply at the arguments produced in favour of the Anabaptist opinion.

II. Dipping not proved by the Scriptures.

Five arguments have been advanced in favour of the doctrine that immersion is essential to baptism, which we take in their natural order:—

1. MEANING OF THE WORD βαπτίζω *(baptizo)*. It is alleged by the Anabaptists that the meaning of this word is *to dip, and nothing but to dip*, and that the word carries this signification with it from the classics into the New Testament.

For sake of argument, we shall suppose it proved that this is the sense of the word in every occurrence. Then, says the Anabaptist, literal compliance with the meaning of the word is essential—to apply water in the form of pouring or sprinkling is not the ordinance. Now, apply this reasoning to the sister ordinance of the Lord's Supper, and see how it looks. The word *supper* means a *full meal*, and a *meal taken at night*. Not only so, but the only detailed accounts of its administration in the Bible show it was observed in the evening. It was instituted on the night when Christ was betrayed, and the sermon that Paul preached on the occasion of its celebration at Troas lasted till midnight. Are we to say, then, that because the word supper means a full meal taken in the evening, that a *small quantity* of bread and wine taken *in the morning* is not the ordinance, and that to call it in such circumstances a *supper* is a burlesque on a divine institution? Did not the very fact that Christ appointed the ordinance *after* the *Paschal* Supper, show that the Lord's *Supper* was never intended to be a full meal, and that, therefore, literal compliance with all expressed in the word *supper* is not essential. Are not all professing Christians, as shown by their practice, unanimous that in observing the ordinance it is not necessary to comply with all that the word *supper* means? Now, *if the literal meaning of the word is not to regulate our observance of the Supper, why should it regulate our observance of Baptism?*

Throughout both ordinances we, at least, act consistently. The design of the Lord's Supper is to exhibit in a symbol the great work of the Lord Jesus: the design of baptism is to exhibit in a symbol the great work of the Holy Spirit in purifying the soul from the filth of sin. Now, as any amount of bread and wine, however small, is enough to figure forth the body and the blood of the Redeemer, so any amount of water, however small, is enough to figure forth the Spirit's cleansing power. The atonement that brings life to the dying sinner is as evidently seen in that piece of bread and drop of wine that we use in the ordinance, as if all the bread in the bakery and all the wine in the cellar were set upon the table; and sanctification, the work of the Holy Ghost upon our polluted nature, is as evidently seen in that handful of water poured on the face of a believer or his child, as if either of them was plunged beneath the Atlantic ocean. We act consistently in each case, never losing sight of the design of each ordinance in our administration of it. But the Anabaptist acts without any consistency whatever. Baptism, he thinks, means dipping, and therefore without dipping there is, in his view, no baptism; but supper, he knows, means an evening meal, nevertheless, he thinks there is no necessity to observe it in the evening, or make a meal of it at all. In the one ordinance, the literal meaning of the word *is* to be carried out; in the other, the literal meaning of the word is *not* to be carried out: in the one, mode with him is everything; in the other, mode is nothing.

But do I grant that *baptizo* means nothing but to dip? Though I have argued on this supposition, *I grant no such thing*. On the contrary, it has been repeatedly shown that the word *baptizo* has not one meaning only, but two in classical writers. It means, first, *to put an object into an element or liquid*; and, taken in this sense, it is a synonym for *dip* or *immerse*, as is admitted on all sides. It means, also, *to put an element or liquid on or over an object*. Our own Dr. Wilson, in common with many others, has proved this secondary sense by the clearest and most convincing examples out of the Greek classics; and those who deny this meaning have no means of escaping from the proof, except by taking refuge in the thicket of figure, which is often a place of convenient retreat for those who find it more easy to evade than to answer an argument.

Two meanings, therefore, being proved in the classic writers, the question arises, which of these meanings does the word retain in the Greek of the New Testament? Does it retain but one, or does it retain them both? It is, of course, well known that in the New Testament we have the Greek language applied to subjects which Pagan writers never dreamed of, and new ideas are expressed, sometimes, indeed, by new words found nowhere else, but far more frequently by the enlargement or limitation of terms already in use. We are not, therefore, warranted to assume that either of the two significations of *baptizo*, which are found in the classics, necessarily attaches to the word in the New Testament, except *it is first proved clearly that the inspired writers actually use it in this sense.* Now, this we are prepared to do for the *secondary* meaning of the word—to produce, at least, one clear case where there was baptism but no immersion. The Apostles at Pentecost were baptized with the Holy Ghost, but were not dipped into Him. The sound as of a mighty wind filled the house, but it was with the Holy Ghost, not with the sound, that they were baptized. The spiritual element, as will be shown more at length hereafter, *was shed forth, fell,* and *came upon* the persons of the Apostles, and, *in consequence of this*, they are said to have been *baptized* with the Holy Ghost. The action expressed by the word here is the putting of the element *upon* the person. Here, then, is our proof that the secondary meaning of the word is carried from the classics into the New Testament. This being proved, we are now entitled to assume that the word in Scripture is *everywhere* used in the same sense, except that *one case equally clear can be produced of a baptism where there must have been immersion.* Till this is proved, the meaning of the word in Scripture is not immersion in a single case. But if one instance from Scripture can be produced where the word *must* mean *immersion,* then we have in proof *two* Scriptural meanings competing with each other, between which nothing but the context can decide. This one instance we maintain no Anabaptist ever has produced, or ever can. Here, then, is how the case stands. Two meanings of the word *baptize* are found in classic writers: of these, one alone is proved to attach to the word in the New Testament, and THAT ONE IS NOT IMMERSION.

It is told of one of the great soldiers of antiquity that, when he could not untie the knot, he drew his sword and cut it. The American Anabaptists have lately performed a similar act of valour. They have made a new version of the

Scripture, and where the word *baptize* occurs in the English Bible, they strike it out and insert the word *immerse*. Such a fact is instructive. They feel that the Bible is not upon their side, else there would be no necessity to mend it. The *dipping* theory must be hard pressed when, in order to maintain it, it is found needful to lay an unholy hand on the Book of God. Uzzah would not have dared to touch the ark, had it not been to avert what seemed to him a great calamity. Dipping is in danger, when men have to tamper with the Bible in order to prove it.

2. THE PRACTICE OF JOHN. We are informed in Matt. iii. 6, how the people "were baptized of him in Jordan," and also in John iii. 23, that he was "baptizing in Ænon near to Salim, because there was much water there." It is alleged that this fact furnishes a strong presumption that dipping was the mode of John's baptism.

It is but fair to say that the presumption would be strong, if this was the only information given in Scripture regarding the *place* of baptism. But it will be found, on examination, that to baptize where there is "much water" was the exception, not the rule. In Acts ii. 41, we find three thousand were baptized in a single day at Jerusalem, where there is no lake, no river, and, during the summer, "much water" of no kind. The citizens of Samaria were baptized (Acts viii. 12) although it does not appear that that city had an abundance of water. The eunuch was baptized in a desert (Acts viii. 26); and, so far as appears from the narrative, Saul of Tarsus had not to leave his lodgings in order to be baptized (Acts ix. 18). The jailer and his family were baptized at midnight in a prison (Acts xvi. 33). With such facts before us, on what side does the presumption lie? Not on the side of dipping, for, confessedly, it requires abundance of water; but on the side of pouring or sprinkling, because it is possible anywhere. In a river, a fountain, a city of persecutors, in a desert, in a prison, or in a private house, it is possible to baptize by putting water upon the person. We never read of the Apostles going forth in quest of water: with them the means for performing baptism is always at hand.

If John baptized in Jordan and in Ænon, there is a reason for it. No house could accommodate the multitude that flocked to hear him. He preached in the open air, and, this being the case, he might as well preach by the river side as anywhere else. In a country so badly watered, it is as serious an offence to trespass on a man's wells as it would be in this country to make free with his orchard, and even when the country was much less populous, interference with wells was a frequent cause of strife (Gen. xxvi. 17-33). John avoided this, and chose a place where there was abundance of water. Water was needed for his baptism, let him administer the rite as he pleased; water was needed for the crowds of people who, under that hot sun, thronged to hear him, and many of whom, we must believe, left home but ill provided; water was needed for the beasts of burden that many would bring with them. The Baptist interfered with no man's rights, and he consulted for the comfort of his hearers when he preached and baptized by the river side. But, to infer from that circumstance that he must of necessity have dipped the people, is to draw upon the imagination.

Let it be remembered that the argument for dipping from the practice of John is a mere inference. But the inference is set aside the moment it can be reasonably suggested that the water may have been needed for other purposes. Even to prove such a suggestion is not essential; the utmost that can be fairly required is to show, as has now been done, that the suggestion is possible and reasonable. Indeed, the mere possibility of the water being needed for other purposes than dipping, is enough to show that dipping is not a necessary inference; and, if the inference from the facts is not necessary, it is ruined as an argument.

To bring the matter to a point. John might have chosen a place well provided with water, *without dipping his hearers; therefore, the fact that he chose such a place, can never prove that he dipped them.*

3. THE BAPTISM OF THE EUNUCH is another of the facts adduced in favour of immersion. The words are found in Act viii. 38-39—"He commanded the chariot to stand still: and they went down both into the water, both Philip and the Eunuch, and he baptized him. And when they were come up out of the water, the Spirit of the Lord caught away Philip." The fact "that they went down both *into* the water," and "came up *out* of the water," is supposed to favour immersion, and is often quoted as if it settled the question.

It will here be noticed that whatever force is in this argument, is found in the use of the prepositions *into* and *out of*. Were it not for them, any other place where baptism is named would be as good an argument for immersion as this. But surely no proof so plausible at sight ever proved so unsatisfactory on examination.

First. It is stated "they went down both into the water, both Philip and the Eunuch." But this surely cannot mean that Philip was dipped. He had been a deacon, and was now a preacher, and it will scarcely be said that on this occasion he dipped himself to keep the Eunuch company. The Anabaptists hold that the Eunuch alone was dipped, and that Philip acted as dipper on the occasion. But if the language does not prove that Philip was dipped, it is hard to see how it can prove that the Eunuch was dipped, for the words from which the argument is drawn are equally applicable to both— "They went down both into the water," and "they came up out of the water." One cannot help asking, if Philip could go "down into the water" and "come up out of the water," without being dipped, why could not the Eunuch do the same?

Secondly. The language used does not necessarily imply that either of them was dipped. The horse every time he drinks at the pond goes *down into* the water, and comes *up out* of the water, but it does not follow from this that he was *under* the water. Had both stood in the pool, and the Eunuch been baptized by the pouring of water on his face or head, the language of the passage would be a correct description of the fact. We lay it down as a self-evident truth, that no argument from circumstances is ever decisive, if any other explanation of the circumstances is proved possible.

To bring this argument to a point. The Eunuch, as well as Philip, could go down *into* the water and come up *out of* the water, *without being dipped; therefore, the fact that he went down into it, and came up out of it, does not prove that he was dipped.*

4. BURIED IN BAPTISM. This argument is founded on Rom. vi. 3-7, and Col. ii. 12. Let both passages, and the context, be examined in the Scriptures, for they are too lengthy to be here transcribed. The words thought to be decisive on the Mode of Baptism are these—"Know ye not, that so many of us as were baptized into Jesus Christ were baptized into His death? Therefore we are buried with Him by baptism into death: that like as Christ was raised up from the dead by the glory of the Father, even so we also should walk in newness of life." The passage in Colossians is of similar import—"Buried with Him in baptism, wherein also ye are risen with Him through the faith of the operation of God, who hath raised Him from the dead." It is argued from these passages, that in baptism there must be the symbol of a burial, and that

as dipping in the water is the only form that resembles burial, therefore the only true mode of baptism is to dip.

If this be the true interpretation of the passages, Paul must have been one of the weakest reasoners who ever tried his hand at logic. For what does it make him say? Turn to that passage in Romans, and you will find that the Apostle is there dealing with the charge, which has been in all ages brought against the doctrines of grace, that they encourage men to live in sin. The Anabaptist would have us believe that Paul meets this charge by alleging that we are dipped in baptism, and because we have been dipped, we are *symbolically* one with Christ in His death, burial, and resurrection, and are, of course, *figuratively* freed from sin. The force of the reasoning thus ascribed to the Apostle may be estimated by a parallel. A charge of ungodliness is brought against the character of, let us say, John Robinson. John meets it after this fashion. He asserts that on last Sabbath he sat at the Lord's table in some place of worship: he states that his partaking of the elements was symbolic of his feeding by faith on the Redeemer: and he alleges farther, that *through the ordinance* he is symbolically one with Christ in His death, and that being thus *symbolically* dead, he is freed from sin and from every other charge. Poor logic, one would say—not very like the logic of Paul. Honest John would soon find that his moral position was not much improved by his symbolic argument.

To show how erroneous it is to understand the Apostle, in Rom. vi. 3, to speak of the baptism of water, we take an illustration from the case of Simon Magus. The sorcerer was baptized by Philip, no doubt, after the most orthodox form (Acts viii. 13) Apply now to the case of Simon the facts stated in Romans vi. According to it, he must have been "*baptized into Jesus Christ—baptized into His death—buried with Christ* by baptism." He must have "*walked in newness of life*;" he must have had his old man "*crucified with Christ;*" and, being dead in Christ, he must have been "freed from sin." Now, if any man can have such blessings by water baptism, water baptism must be of more value than even Anabaptists think it. But that Simon, though baptized by Philip, received no such benefits as these "by baptism," is evident from the words afterwards addressed to him by Peter—"I perceive that thou art in the gall of bitterness, and in the bond of iniquity." A rather odd sort of address to a man who, if the Anabaptist interpretation of Romans vi. is correct, must have been baptized into Jesus Christ, and who, of course, being dead and buried with Christ by baptism, must have been freed from sin!

Light makes darkness disappear: a plain statement of the truth is the best way to scatter clouds of error. The error in the Anabaptist interpretation of Rom. vi. 3, and Col. ii. 12, arises from understanding the word *baptism* to apply to the external ordinance as administered by man, whereas it refers to the gift of the Spirit as dispensed by God. To the illustration of the passages we bring I Cor. xii. 13— "For by one Spirit are we all baptized into one body, whether we be Jews or Gentiles, bond or free." Apart from the bestowment of miraculous powers, there is a baptism of the Spirit that introduces a sinner into the body of Christ. This baptism produces faith in the human soul: faith unites us to Jesus, and makes us members of His body, of His flesh, and of His bones (Eph. v.30) Being thus members of His own body, we are one with Christ our head, in His death, burial, resurrection, and glory. Though a man were dipped in Jordan itself, it never can in reality be said of him, till he is baptized with the Spirit, that he is crucified with Christ, or buried with Christ, or risen with Christ, or that he sits in heavenly places with Christ. Here, then, is the Apostle's reasoning, in our view; grace, he maintains, does not encourage men to live in sin; for grace brings its subjects into union with Christ, and, baptized by the Holy Ghost, they are brought into such close relationship to Jesus, that being members of His body, they suffer on His cross, die in His death, lie in His grave, and share in His glory. All who partake of such a baptism, are, of course, dead with Christ, and freed from sin. This is sound reasoning; but to say that the doctrines of grace do not countenance a life of sin, merely because a man in his baptism with water received *the symbol* of such blessings, is to make the Apostle speak, if not nonsense, at least nothing to the purpose.

As the passages in question refer to the *effects* that follow the baptism of the Spirit, it is obvious that no argument can be drawn from them as to the *manner* in which the baptism of water is to be administered. Men are buried with Christ, not by being dipped in water by a poor frail mortal like themselves, but by the Holy Ghost baptizing their souls, and producing in them that faith which connects the soul with Christ, both in His death and in His life. No wonder that many of the more ignorant Anabaptists think that to be dipped is to be saved, when they are taught that by water baptism they are buried with Christ and rise with Him to newness of life. Can they, under such teaching, be very much blamed, if they believe that a soul dead and risen with Christ is in no danger, and if they think that, as dipping secures this, dipping is salvation? But our doctrine—namely, that where the baptism of the Spirit is union with Christ, pardon, holiness, and heaven follow after—is a doctrine in obvious harmony with all Divine revelation.

5. THE PRACTICE OF THE EARLY CHURCH. There can be no doubt that in the age immediately after the Apostles, as we learn from the Greek Fathers, immersion was the ordinary way of administering baptism. But much importance cannot be attached to this by any who consider how early errors in doctrine, government, and worship sprang up in the primitive Church. Even when the Apostles were alive, the mystery of iniquity was at work: forms and ceremonies, having no foundation in Scripture, rapidly multiplied, and many errors in worship and doctrine were in full bloom in the second century. That immersion was practised by the Christians of that time is no more than can be said for the sign of the cross, and anointing with oil, in connexion with the baptismal ordinance. It is dangerous to plead the practice of the primitive Church for anything which has no foundation in the Scripture. Church history is not the rule of a Christian's faith. We care little that immersion has a footing in antiquity, so long as it has no footing in the Bible.

Here, then, is the utmost that can be established about dipping. To dip is one of the two meanings of *baptizo* in classical Greek, and Christians in the second century, after the death of the Apostles, are known to have baptized by immersion. Whatever countenance these two facts give to dipping, dipping enjoys. But it detracts seriously from the weight of these facts that neither of them are Scriptural arguments. It cannot be proved that the word retains its primary meaning in Scripture, nor can it be proved that the practice of the Church in the second century was the practice of the Apostles of Christ. The proofs alleged from Scripture turn out, on examination, to be no proofs whatsoever. In the whole Word of God there is no command to dip. There is no example in Scripture of any one whatever, of whom it can be proved that he was dipped in baptism. All the evidence adduced from Scripture, and we never heard of any other than that already stated, is only a variety of circumstances which, at the first blush, favour dipping, but which, when carefully examined, say nothing definite on the subject. Yet this is the sort of evidence 0n which the Anabaptist rests his notion about dipping, and founds his assertion that every other Christian is unbaptized. The weaker his argument, the bolder his tone; and, this being so, little wonder that he is loud and bold indeed.

III. The Scriptural Mode of Baptism.

The candid inquirer, anxious to know the truth, may now be supposed to put the question, If dipping cannot be proved by the Bible, is there any other mode of baptism which can plead the authority of God? This question can be answered to the satisfaction of every unprejudiced man. There is quite enough in the New Testament to show all that was required in order to constitute a valid baptism.

Be it remembered, that the exact point now to be determined is, *How* is a baptism to be effected? Is it by a person being put *into* the element, or is it by the element being put *upon* the person? The *manner* in which the person and the element *come in contact* is the exact point to be ascertained. Now, the Word of God determines this nice question for us.

The key to the understanding of the whole subject is found in Matt. iii. 11—"I indeed baptize you with water unto repentance: but He that cometh after me is mightier than I, whose shoes I am not worthy to bear: HE SHALL BAPTIZE YOU WITH THE HOLY GHOST, AND WITH FIRE." This prophecy of John, as all agree, found its fulfilment at Pentecost, when the Holy Ghost was poured out upon them, and they were endowed with the gift of tongues and other miraculous powers. Premising this, and anxious that the reader should keep before his mind the verse now quoted, let us turn, in the first place, to—

Acts i. 8.—Here we find the Lord Jesus speaking to His disciples immediately before His ascension. He commands them (verse 4) not to depart from Jerusalem, but to wait for the promise of the Father: that promise, in ver. 5, He explains to be the baptism of the Holy Ghost; and He goes on to say (verse 8), "Ye shall receive power after that the Holy Ghost is COME UPON you: and ye shall be witnesses unto me both in Jerusalem, and in all Judæa," &c. Mark that word, *come upon*; for it expresses mode. The way in which the Apostles were baptized was by the Holy Ghost *coming upon* them. The result of the Spirit coming upon the Apostles, was their baptism with the Spirit. We conclude from this, that when the water of the ordinance comes upon people, it results in their baptism with water.

Acts ii. 3.—The day of Pentecost had now fully come; the disciples were together in one place: suddenly a sound from heaven as of a rushing wind filled the house where they were sitting, and, as we read in verse 3, "there appeared unto them cloven tongues like as of fire, and it SAT UPON each of them." The tongue of fire *sitting on* each of them is almost universally regarded as the fulfilment of the promise—"He shall baptize you with fire." There is a mixed metaphor, no doubt, in speaking of fire *sitting*, as the Evangelist does; but that does not prevent the word from showing very conclusively the *mode* of the baptism. The Apostles were not dipped into the fire, but the fire *sat upon* them. They were not put into the element, the element was put upon them. Consequently, when water is put *upon* the person, there is a Scriptural baptism, but no immersion. The term used indicates clearly the mode of administration. If the fire sitting on the disciples constituted the baptism of fire, then the water of the ordinance resting on the person constitutes the baptism of water.

Acts ii. 17.—That same day Peter addressed the multitude, and explained to them the extraordinary event which had so recently occurred. This, he says, was what might have been expected. One of the ancient prophets had long since said that in the latter days God would pour out His Spirit on all flesh; and the present baptism, he would have them understand, is only the first fulfilment of that ancient promise—"And it shall come to pass in the last days, saith God, I will POUR OUT of my Spirit upon all flesh." Mark that word—*pour out;* for it determines mode. Now, I ask, if the pouring out of the Spirit is the true mode of administering the baptism of the Spirit, is not the pouring out of water in the ordinance the mode of administering the baptism of water?

Acts ii. 33.—Towards the conclusion of the same discourse Peter again speaks of the Spirit, the promise of whom the Lord Jesus had received from the Father, and he says it was this Holy Ghost whom an exalted Saviour had bestowed—"Therefore being by the right hand of God exalted, and having received of the Father the promise of the Holy Ghost, He hath SHED FORTH this, which ye now see and hear." Mark the word—*shed forth*; for it expresses mode, and embodies the fulfilment of the promise, "He shall baptize you with the Holy Ghost." I ask, again, when the shedding forth of the Holy Ghost results in the baptism of the Holy Ghost, why should not the shedding forth of water in the ordinance result in the baptism of water?

Acts xi. 15, 16.—Peter, on returning to Jerusalem, after admitting the first Gentile believers to the Church, is called to account for his conduct in associating with the heathen, and, in self-defence, he rehearses the whole affair which had lately taken place in Cesarea. He recounted the matter from the beginning, and at verse 15 he says, "As I began to speak, the Holy Ghost FELL ON them, as on us at the beginning. Then remembered I the word of the Lord how that He said, John indeed baptized with water; but ye shall be baptized with the Holy Ghost." In the Holy Ghost falling on them, Peter saw the fulfilment of the promise, "He shall baptize you with the Holy Ghost." That word, *fell*, is worth your notice; for it expresses mode. We ask the candid reader to answer this question—If the Holy Ghost's falling on persons is the true mode of the baptism of the Holy Ghost, why should not the water of the ordinance, falling upon persons, be the true mode of the baptism of water?

This Pentecostal Baptism, administered by God Himself, will be forever conclusive as to the Scriptural mode of baptism. The most ignorant reader, if gifted with the very slightest power of thought, cannot fail to see that the Apostles were not dipped into the Spirit, nor plunged into the Spirit, but that the Spirit was shed forth, poured out, fell on them, came upon them, sat upon them, and, *in consequence of this, they are said to be baptized with the Holy Ghost.* These different terms show the mode in which the element and they came, so to speak, into contact, and that is the very point which we desire to know.

It is in vain to attempt to escape the force of this argument by saying that this baptism was spiritual. We answer, it was a real and true baptism; the element, indeed, was spiritual, but that does not prevent us from seeing *the mode in which the person and the element came into contact with each other,* and that is all which at present we care for seeing. It has been said that this was a figurative baptism; but, even admitting it to be so, the figurative always rests on the basis of the literal, and the language used is only justified by the fact that the literal baptism is produced by water *coming upon* the person. Had it been otherwise, how easy would it have been to have filled the house with the Spirit before the entrance of the Apostles, to thrust them into the house, and then to speak of them as dipped in the Spirit or plunged in the Spirit. That He did otherwise, will for ever be proof that baptism is possible without immersion.

This is surely enough for any one who wishes to know the mind of God on the mode. The reader can now judge for himself what is the Scriptural form. Let it be observed, that in our positive argument we rest nothing on mere circumstances, which might, perhaps, be capable of another explanation. We are content to allow God, in His own Word, to speak for Himself. We consult the oracle which never fails, believing that the best interpreter of Scripture is the Scripture itself. By five distinct words, we are informed of the Scriptural mode of baptism. When the Holy Ghost is shed forth, is poured out, falls, comes upon, or rests on persons, they are baptized with the Holy Ghost: we conclude, therefore, when the water of the ordinance is shed forth, poured out, falls, comes upon, or rests on persons, that they are baptized with water. The baptism, then, which the Scripture recognizes, is the *putting of water on the person*, not the putting of the person into the water. Nothing can be proved from the Bible if this is not proved, that A MAN IS SCRIPTURALLY BAPTIZED WHEN THE BAPTIZING ELEMENT IS PUT UPON HIM.

IV. Conclusion.

In our second chapter, it has been shown that there is, in reality, no proof from Scripture in favour of immersion. To the reader, as well as to ourselves, this, we hope, is now evident. But let us suppose for a moment that in this we are mistaken—that there is some latent force in the evidence that has failed to reach us, and that immersion is in proof as a Scriptural mode. What would follow logically from this?

Not that dipping is the only mode of Scriptural administration, but that we have two modes, one by putting the person into the water, the other by putting water upon the person. In this case, dipping would stand on a level with what we have shown to be the Scriptural mode. To prove that baptism by immersion is right, never can prove that baptism by pouring is wrong; even as to show that the attitude of standing in prayer is right, never can prove that the attitude of kneeling is wrong. Men might be left to choose between two modes of baptism, as they are left to choose between two postures in prayer, both of which are sanctioned by Scripture example. S0 that a man might admit all the arguments advanced by the Anabaptist from the Scripture in favour of his practice, and yet refuse to admit that dipping is essential to the ordinance; because, notwithstanding such an admission, it would be still in proof that the disciples were baptized in a different form.

Now, this is the position that perhaps the great majority of professing Christians have actually adopted on this question. They see, as they think, evidence in the Bible for two modes, dipping and pouring: they believe that it is a matter of very small importance which of these is adopted, because, in either case, there is the washing of water; and where there is the washing of water, there is all, so far as mode is concerned, which is essential to the ordinance. This is the view of the matter taken by the most influential of the Protestant Churches. The Church of England gives to the officiating clergyman the choice of dipping or pouring, according to circumstances. The Presbyterian Church does not condemn dipping; what it says upon the mode is that "dipping is not *necessary*, but baptism is rightly administered by sprinkling." B0th Churches leave an option to the minister to adopt the one or the other mode according to circumstances: they carefully refrain from saying that either the one mode or the other is *essential* to the ordinance. Hosts of eminent writers take the same view of the question.

Now, of these well-known facts Anabaptist writers are constantly taking an unfair advantage. They find many theologians who admit that dipping was an ancient and a Scriptural mode of baptism, just as they believe pouring to have been an ancient and a Scriptural mode. In these circumstances, one of the most common devices of Anabaptist writers (I mean, of course, the smaller fry—such men as Carson were above it), is to extract sentences from the works of Pædobaptist writers, in which they speak favourably of immersion, taking good care to conceal, at the same time, that these writers believed that baptism by pouring was no less Scriptural and valid. They seek to convey the impression to the unwary and ignorant, by quoting half-truths from great authors, that the whole Christian world is on their side, only that from some unworthy motives they did not act up to their convictions. Whereas, the truth is, that perhaps not a single man of all those whose opinions are thus quoted, held the Anabaptist doctrine that dipping is *essential* to baptism. They held, most of them, that the two modes are equally Scriptural, equally right, and equally valid; but the Anabaptist, instead of telling this, quotes *only* what they say in favour of dipping, leaves what they say for the other mode unquoted, and thus misrepresents their testimony. No writer of eminence in any Church holds, or I believe ever held, the doctrine that a *man undipped is a man unbaptized* —the Anabaptist, of course, always excepted. He alone says, no dip—no baptism.

None except the grossly ignorant can ever be swayed by mere human opinion in matters of religion. Men who have not carefully examined a matter are always the most ready to make admissions; and if they have attained eminence in any other way, these admissions, made often after a very slight examination of the case, are at all times liable to be flung in our faces. But, apart from the reasons on which they rest, human opinion goes for little with men who make the Scripture alone the rule of their faith. "Let God be true, and every man a liar." We have no wish but to know the mind of God upon the matter, as expressed in His own Word. The conclusion to which *we* arrive on the whole subject is, that if we look only at the design of baptism to furnish a symbol of sanctification, either dipping or sprinkling will do, because, in either case, there is the washing of water. If the rule of faith were the classics and the Fathers, dipping would have more abundant proofs in its favour than sprinkling; but if we are to be guided by the Scripture alone, the only mode of baptism which *can be proved by it* is that of PUTTING WATER UPON THE PERSON.

THE SUBJECTS OF BAPTISM.

WE now proceed to a department of the doctrine which all allow is of much more importance than that which has hitherto been under discussion. We mean an inquiry into the *Subjects of Baptism*. Christians, it is to be lamented, are not entirely at one even on the question, *Who should be baptized*? Here, too, human infirmity fails, we think, to apprehend the full testimony of God, and Anabaptism commits the error of denying one-half of the truth. It shall be our business to set before the reader the essential facts of the case, to bring out clearly the points of agreement and of difference, and to exhibit the evidence so as to enable each man to judge for himself what the Scripture really testifies on the matter.

I. The Question in Debate.

In all sound reasoning, the first thing is to know accurately the point in debate. In no controversy was it ever more needed than in this. The Anabaptists invariably represent that believer baptism is their doctrine, and that infant baptism is ours. This representation is both unfair and unfounded; but, with them, it is a favourite mode of stating the question, because it enables them to parade a great number of texts to prove that believers were baptized in apostolic times—a fact which, of course, nobody denies—and then to call upon us to produce an equal array in proof that infants were baptized. The design, of course, is to convey to the unsuspecting reader the impression that all the Scripture is on their side, and no Scripture against them. In vain any man attempts to set them right—they seem to have no desire to be set right. The next day they will inform the public that they hold the baptism of believers, and that we hold the baptism of infants. Such a represcutation is a proof of weakness; any cause that is strong and true never wilfully misstates the case.

What is the real state of the matter? Plainly this, that the baptism of believers, *in the circumstances described in the Scriptures,* is as much the doctrine of any other Protestant Church as it is the doctrine of the Anabaptists, the only difference between them and us, on the subjects of baptism, being simply, *whether the ordinance ought to be administered to the infant children of believers.*

The baptism of believers is, we repeat, common ground to us and them. Every instance recorded in Scripture of faith being required in order to baptism, is a case where *we* would require faith in order to baptism. The 3000 at Pentecost (Acts ii. 41), Saul of Tarsus (Acts ix. 18) and the disciples at Ephesus (Acts xix. 5), were, up to that period, Jews, who, on entering into the Christian Church, were baptized, after making a profession of faith, but who would not have received the ordinance from us on any other terms. The same condition, previous to baptism, we would have demanded from the Eunuch (Acts viii. 35), from Cornelius and his friends (Acts x. 47), and from Lydia (Acts xvi. 15)—for they were Jewish proselytes asking admission into the Christian Church. Simon Magus and his fellow-townsmen (Acts viii. 12, 13) believed and were baptized; but these Samaritans—the adherents of a false and corrupt worship—would not by us have been taken into the Church without baptism, nor baptized without faith. The jailer of Philippi (Acts xvi. 33,34), and the Corinthians (Acts xviii. 8, and I Cor. i. 13-17) were previously heathens, who had to believe before being baptized, and on no other terms would such persons be admitted to membership in any Evangelical Church. These are all the cases recorded in the Scriptures where faith preceded baptism; and any one of all is enough to prove that any person, *in the same circumstances as they were,* must believe in order to be baptized. But mark what these circumstances were:—every one of them, up to the period of his baptism, was either a Jew or a Jewish proselyte, a Samaritan or a heathen; every one of them was an adult, coming into the Christian Church from the world beyond it; every one of them was the case of a person whose parents had not been Christians; and none of them had ever received Christian baptism before. There is no Protestant Church in Christendom that would not require faith from all of them prior to baptism; because, from the day that the Christian Church was founded, they were all, without exception, out of the visible Church, and our doctrine has always been, that "baptism is not to be administered to any that are out of the visible Church, *till they profess their faith in Christ and obedience to Him"* (Shorter Catechism, Quest. 95). The baptism of believers, in such circumstances as the Scripture prescribes, being the doctrine of our Church, patent on the face of its standards for ages, the Anabaptists have no more right to quote these Scripture examples against us than we have to quote these examples against them; and, however it may prop up a sect, it can never serve the interests of truth to represent, as they invariably do, that the baptism of believers is exclusively their doctrine, and not ours.

Let there be no mistake on this subject with the reader. We maintain that, when any one, born *beyond the membership* of the Christian Church, whether a Pagan, a Samaritan, or a Jew, would seek admission within its pale, he cannot be baptized till he believes. On this part of the subject both sides are agreed. We only differ from the Anabaptist when he argues that, because an adult needs faith before baptism, therefore an infant needs faith before baptism. His logic does not seem to us convincing, when he maintains, because a profession of faith was needed from Jews, Samaritans, and Pagans on their entrance into the Church, therefore the infants of those in church-membership already need to make a profession of faith, or be excluded from baptism for want of it. If faith before baptism is required from adults in certain circumstances, it seems to us poor reasoning to argue, from that fact, that faith before baptism is required from infants in totally different circumstances. A foreigner, who means to settle in our islands, requires to take out letters of naturalization before he can claim the rights of a British subject; but it does not, therefore follow that one who is British-born requires to do the same. Anabaptists think that the same qualification is required for the child of a church member, previous to its baptism, as is required from an unbaptized adult 0n his admission to the Church, and exclude infants from baptism for want of this qualification. We, on the contrary, think that, to refuse a child baptism, on the ground that it does not possess a qualification which the Scripture does not require from a child, is both unscriptural and unjust.

What, then, is the precise point in dispute? Not the baptism of believers, because the baptism of believers, in all such circumstances as those specified in Scripture, is common ground. The point on which we differ is simply this, *What is to be done with the infant children of Church members?* We say, "Recognise their Church membership by baptism." "No," says the Anabaptist, "leave them unbaptized till they understand the Gospel, and make a profession of faith for themselves." The difference regards children only; and every argument that does not bear on this particular point is out of place on either side.

II. Anabaptist Objections.

That infant baptism is the practice of all branches of the Christian Church, with one solitary exception, is a well-known fact. That it has been the practice of the Church of God for eighteen centuries is also beyond dispute. When one sect, therefore, ventures to differ in opinion from all other Christian Churches, it should have very strong reasons to support it. Let us consider the objections which they advance against the administration of the ordinance to the children of believers, and then let all men judge whether they are sound and conclusive.

1. The first of these objections is founded on the *baptism of Christ*—Matt. iii. 13-17. The fact that Christ was not baptized in childhood, but only when he entered on his ministry, some thirty years afterwards, is considered by many of the more ignorant class a strong proof against infant baptism.

My answer to this will be short. At the time of Christ's birth, the ordinance of baptism did not exist in the Church of God. Circumcision was then the initiatory rite, and Christ was circumcised (Luke ii. 21). Thirty years afterwards, John was sent to baptize, and so soon as the opportunity presented itself, Christ submitted to the rite. But although His own disciples baptized during the Saviour's lifetime (John iv. 1, 2), yet it was not till the Lord had risen from the dead that Christian baptism was instituted (Matt. xxviii. 19). The mere fact, therefore, that the Lord Jesus did not receive, in infancy, an ordinance that did not exist till after His death and resurrection, is surely no argument against infant baptism. One might as well argue against the circumcision of infants, on the ground that Abraham was not circumcised till he was a hundred years of age.

2. Again, it is said, that an *infant cannot understand baptism*, and eloquent pictures are sometimes drawn of the wrong inflicted on the poor unconscious babe which receives an ordinance of which it knows nothing, and is made a party to a solemn transaction without any consent of its own.

It is admitted, readily, that a child at baptism does not understand the nature of the ordinance of which it is the subject, but that is no reason why it should not derive benefit thereby. It does not know the texture of the clothes that cover it, and yet these clothes keep it warm. It does not understand the nature of its mother's milk, and yet that milk sustains its life. The children that were brought to Jesus that He might touch them (Mark x. 13-16), did not understand the ceremony that was gone through on that occasion, and yet we cannot but believe that Christ's blessing did them good. An Anabaptist might have rebuked those mothers, and said to them, "Take your children home, what is the good of it? What can they know about Christ's blessing?" But Jesus would have shown him, what he did show the ignorant disciples, that with such conduct He "was *much displeased.*" A Divine purpose may be served, and good may be done, by the administration of baptism to a child, while, at the same time, the child does not understand the ordinance. If our Anabaptist friends had seen a Jew, with knife in hand, ready to perform on an infant of eight days old the rite of circumcision, they would have attempted to dissuade him from his bloody work in some such way as this—"How can this poor babe know anything of a covenant made so many years ago? Why administer to it an ordinance that it does not understand? Why make it a party to such a solemn transaction without any consent of its own?" The Jew could scarcely hide his contempt for one so ignorant of the Law and the Prophets, as he would reply—"Beautiful reasoning, indeed, thou Gentile unbeliever! but with me it does not weigh one feather against the appointment of God." Now, we say the same. The baptized infant may be ignorant of the ordinance, but that does not, with us, weigh one feather against the appointment of God. Dr. Carson, an Anabaptist writer, says, "I would baptize Satan himself, without the smallest scruple, had I a Divine warrant."[1] Possessing, as we do, a Divine warrant for baptizing the children of believers, we hesitate still less to administer the ordinance to an unconscious babe.

3. Again, we are told there is no command or example in the Scriptures for infant baptism.

This would be a fair and honest objection if advanced by persons who themselves renounce every practice that cannot produce from Scripture

---

[1] *Baptism*, p. 196.

express example or command. The parties, however, that state this objection, know very well that in the Word of God there is no command or example for Sabbath Schools, or for admitting females to the Lord's Supper. Both these things, however, are practised by themselves, doubtless for reasons they consider sufficient; and yet they come to ask for our practice a kind of warrant that they are not able to produce for their own. Now, is this fair? Is it reasonable for them to demand for infant baptism evidence of a different kind from that which satisfies them in regard to other practices they acknowledge to be scriptural?

I have often been amused to hear some zealous Anabaptist, breast-high for doing nothing for which express command or example is not forthcoming, undertake to prove one of the practices of his denomination—namely, that females have a right to be admitted to the Lord's Supper. Command he has none. Example he has none. But instantly he enters on the field of inference in some such way as this: he finds it written that "the disciples came together to break bread," and because women are disciples as well as men," he *infers* their right to the communion from the fact of their discipleship. He discovers that females were in the Corinthian Church, to which Paul delivered the ordinance of the Lord's Supper, and thus, from the fact of their membership, he *infers* their right to communion. He ascertains that they came together with the males into one place when the ordinance was about to be observed, and from the fact of their assembling at the same time with the other members, he *infers* the propriety of admitting them to the table. Or, because "a man" is commanded to examine himself prior to partaking of the feast, he *infers* that in the term *man* the female is also included. Thus his argument for female communion is inference throughout; but the moment that he turns to speak of infant baptism, perhaps the very same man will scout inference altogether. Nothing but express precept or example will do now. The very same kind of proof that satisfies him in the one case, will not, in the other, satisfy him at all. Now, let any honest man say whether this is reasonable. The admission of females to the Supper is at least as important as the admission of infants to baptism, and what right has any one to demand for the latter evidence of a different nature from that which is held sufficient in regard to the former? We undertake to maintain the right of infants to baptism with stronger arguments than it is possible to produce for the admission of females to the Lord's

Supper. Our arguments may, in a large degree, be inferential, but it is only an ignorant and shallow reasoner who would object to them on that ground. All that any man has a right to ask is, that our inferences be clear, and sound, and conclusive. On this point most men will agree with an Anabaptist writer already mentioned, who says, "I do not object to inference; on the contrary, I receive what is made out by inference, just as I receive the most direct statement. But an inference is not a guess, or conjecture, or probability, or conceit drawn at random; it must be the necessary result of the principle from which it is deduced." After such a statement, from such a quarter, it would be almost heresy in an Anabaptist to object to inference, more particularly as we engage that any inference we draw shall be the necessary result of the principle from which it is deduced.

4. The most common objection to the baptism of children is, that faith is necessary to baptism, and that as infants cannot believe, they should not be baptized.

The Anabaptist uses no argument that he thinks so powerful and convincing as this. Yet it is the merest sophism, that ought to impose on no man who knows what reasoning is. Such an argument, if sound, would overturn what all admit to be truths. Try it, for example, on the subject of the salvation of infants, and see the result to which it leads. Thus, faith is necessary to salvation; but infants cannot believe, therefore, infants cannot be saved. All candid men must admit that faith is as necessary to salvation as it is to baptism, and if the want of faith shuts an infant out of the Church, the want of faith also shuts an infant out of heaven. It follows, then, that infants dying in infancy are lost. But the possibility of infant salvation is an admitted truth; an argument, therefore, which proves against an admitted truth cannot be a sound argument.

That the reader may see and judge for himself how identical the argument is, I append both cases, so that they may be under his eye at the same time:—

No. 1.	No. 2.
He that believeth and is baptized shall be saved (Mark xvi. 16.)	He that believeth not shall be damned (Mark xvi. 16).
But the infant cannot believe;	But the infant cannot believe;
Therefore,	Therefore,
The infant is not to be baptized.	The infant shall be damned.

We pronounce the conclusion *in both instances* to be false—utterly and awfully false. But the Anabaptist maintains that the conclusion in No. 1 is true, and that the conclusion in No. 2 alone is false. It lies on him, therefore, to show, if he can, how the *same argument* can conduct to a true conclusion in the one case, and a false conclusion in the other. Surely there is no room for evasion here; the major premise is, in both cases, a sentence from the Word of God; the minor premise in the one is identical with that in the other, and, moreover, is admitted to be true by all parties; and the conclusion is drawn exactly in the same way in both cases. If the argument, therefore, is valid against infant baptism, it is equally valid against infant salvation; but if it be a false argument against infant salvation, it is equally false against infant baptism.

The fallacy here arises simply from this cause, that there is more in the conclusion than there is in the premises. When the Scripture speaks of faith as necessary to baptism and to salvation, it speaks with reference to adults only, for such, alone, are capable of faith. The argument takes for granted that an infant needs to possess, for baptism and for salvation, the same qualification as an adult does—that is, must have faith, of which it is known to be incapable. And it concludes that, for want of faith, the infant is entitled neither to baptism nor salvation. But what the Anabaptist requires to prove is, *that God demands the same qualification from an infant as He does from an adult.* Without this, his objection to the baptism of an infant, on the ground that it cannot believe, is not worth a groat. We maintain that faith is not required from an infant, either in order to its baptism or to its salvation. A just God will not demand from a child a qualification of which it is, from the very nature of the case, incapable. If an adult does not believe, he cannot be baptized but it is very different with an infant. If an adult does not believe, he cannot be saved; but it is very different with an infant. Faith is not required in an infant in order to salvation, and faith is not required in an infant in order to baptism. An infant enjoys the privilege of being saved without faith, and of being baptized without faith.

It were well that those, who speak of the want of faith as being a sufficient cause for excluding children from baptism, would attend to the following statement of the late Dr. Carson—"That necessity of faith which the Scriptures apply to *adults, and to adults only*, theologians have applied to infants, without warrant, as if God was bound to proceed towards them as He does towards adults."[2] That sentence is well worthy of remark. He there condemns, as a grand mistake in theologians, the habit of supposing that, because faith is necessary to the salvation of an adult, it must also be necessary to the salvation of an infant. In this we quite agree with him; but we cannot help asking, at the same time, is not this the very mistake that he and his party make in regard to infant baptism? Do they not argue, one and all, that, because faith is necessary to the baptism of an adult, therefore it is necessary to the baptism of an infant? Do they not exclude infants from baptism on the ground that they do not *believe*—on the ground that they do not possess a qualification which the Word of God requires from adults only? May we not apply his own words to himself "That necessity of faith which the Scriptures apply to adults, and to adults only, [Anabaptist] theologians have applied to infants, *without warrant*, as if God was bound to proceed towards them as he does towards adults." The Anabaptist, therefore, is condemned from his own mouth. He acts "without warrant" when he demands faith from an infant in order to baptism; or, what is the same thing, excludes it from baptism for want of faith.

These are the strongest objections that we remember to have heard alleged against infant baptism. Let every unprejudiced man decide whether there is one of them that has not been fully and fairly answered. This being the case, we are now to inquire what amount of evidence Scripture furnishes in its favour. It will not require very much to turn the beam, for as we have seen, there is literally nothing in the opposite scale.

III. Evidence for Infant Baptism.

The great principle that forms the basis on which the practice of baptizing infants rests, is the near and intimate relationship which, by the very constitution of our nature, must ever exist between parent and child. The child partakes of the very nature of the parent; the life of the one is continued in the other, and the interests of both are the same. In a variety of cases, by the very necessity of nature, the act of the parent is justly regarded as the act of the

---

[2] *Baptism*, p. 215.

child. If the parent rise to citizenship in the land of his adoption, his children are considered as having done the same; if the parent renounce one religion and attach himself to another, the child is counted with him. In all such cases, the parent represents his child, and acts on his behalf; and the child, moreover, must be regarded as approving his parent's conduct, until he is in a position to act for himself. This principle, there can be no doubt, has its foundation both in nature and in reason, and, in many cases, it is acted on in the ordinary transactions of life.

Better still—the principle that the parent represents the child, is one that has the repeated sanction and approval of God Himself. Over and over again, children have been parties to those covenants into which it has pleased the Lord to enter with men. In the covenant of works, Adam acted for all his posterity; in the covenant of grace, Christ undertook for all His seed. In both alike, children have their place; over them, as well as others, "sin hath reigned unto death," and over them, too, "grace reigns through righteousness unto eternal life." The covenant with Noah embraced the patriarch and his seed (Gen. ix. 9). The covenant with Abraham did the same (Gen. xvii. 10). The covenant made between God and Israel on the plains of Moab, and which was only a renewal of the covenant at Sinai (Exod. xxiv. 7,8), included the little ones as well as the full grown men and women, they all promising to keep God's covenant, and God promising to be their God (Deut. xxix. 9-13). This latter passage is of great importance, inasmuch as it exhibits parents entering into covenant for themselves and their children and promising obedience. Here we have the clearest sanction to the principle that the parent represents the child while the child is unable to act on its own behalf: that when the parent takes God to be his God, and promises obedience to His commandments, he does for his child what he does for himself; and that till such times as the child becomes a responsible agent, and disowns the act of his parents, "he is not only bound by the parent's act, but is to be regarded and treated as though he had done in his own person what his parent did in his name."[3] Having thus seen that the great principle which lies at the foundation of infant baptism, takes origin in the constitution of our nature, and has been repeatedly recognized in God's covenant dealings with men, I remark:—

---

[3] Article in *Princeton Review*, from which the substance of the two preceding paragraphs is taken.

1. That the infant children of God's people were acknowledged by a religious ordinance to be within the covenant, and in visible membership with the Church of God, for nearly two thousand years before the coming of Christ. The ordinance that recognized this membership was circumcision, which, as all know, was administered to infant children (Gen. xvii. 10; xxi. 4). Circumcision introduced the subject of it to religious privileges; it brought him within a covenant which contained the promise of spiritual blessings (Gen. xvii. 7); it enabled him to eat the passover (Exod. xii. 48), to enter the sanctuary (Ezek. xliv. 9) and to be reckoned with God's professing people: the want of circumcision, on the other hand, was enough to make an Israelite an excommunicated man, "cut off from his people" for breaking the covenant of God (Gen. xvii. 14). It was not administered to the infants of Israel as a mark of carnal descent, to which they were entitled as being the seed of Abraham, as may be seen from these two facts; *first*, that the Ishmaelites, Edomites, and Midianites were the lineal descendants of Abraham, but had no right to the seal of God's covenant on their flesh and, *second*, that the stranger within their gates, in whose veins the blood of Abraham never flowed, might partake in it, and thus profess faith and obedience towards the God of Israel. But infants were circumcised as being the children of God's professing people: and circumcision was the religious rite by which their interest in the covenant and membership in the Church were recognised. It was the outward mark that distinguished God's professing people from the heathen, and it gave the person who received it a right to participate in some of the holiest rites of the ancient religion. That it continued to be the practice to acknowledge, by this ordinance, the membership of infants in the visible Church, down to the advent of Christ, is evident from the fact that, even when the sun of the Old Dispensation was setting, John the Baptist and the Lord Jesus himself were circumcised (Luke i. 59; ii. 21). We hold it proved, therefore, *that the infants of God's professing people, in common with their parents, were recognised members of the Church for nearly 2000 years.*

3. The Church, into whose membership infants were introduced by an express appointment of God, is the same in all essential particulars with the Church that now exists. The Church, as it is in the sight of God, is the collective company of all true saints: the Church, as it is in the sight of men, is the collective company of all who profess the true religion, and their children.

Since the day that the first promise of redemption was given, this, which we call the Church visible, runs through all ages. Dispensations, ordinances, and forms change; but the Church in its membership does not change—it always is the collective company of God's professing people and their children. True religion, in its essence, is always the same—faith in God, and practice corresponding to that faith. The religion of a saint in Jewish times was, in all essential particulars, that of a true Christian now. All who attended to the ordinances, and thereby gave expression to their love and obedience to God, were counted God's people then as now: the true Israel then, as now, were those who repented, found mercy, and lived by faith (Heb. xi): the plan of salvation was the same: the code of morals, as summed up in the ten commandments, was the same: the experience of a servant of God, as may be seen in the Psalms, was the same as at present: and the promises and truths that cheered and instructed them as they passed on upon their way to the promised land, are still supplying green pastures to the flock of Christ as they pass through the wilderness.

At the death and resurrection of Christ, His Church in the world assumed a new form and organization, suited to the altered circumstances in which it was in future to be placed. The civil code that was peculiar to the Jews as a nation, ceased to bind, now that the people of God were no longer to be limited to a nation. The ceremonial law was abolished, for it had found its fulfilment in Jesus. Victims were to be laid on the altar no more, now that the Great Sacrifice was offered. The high priest had no longer need to enter within the vail, now that the Great High Priest had passed into the heavens. Even circumcision itself waxes old and disappears: henceforth, "in Christ Jesus neither circumcision availeth anything, nor uncircumcision, but a new creature." Such a change passed on the Church as passes on the tree, when it sheds the leaves of autumn, old and sere, and the leaves of spring, young and fresh, return: or as passes on the soldier, when he divests himself of his uniform and dresses in plain clothes. The man is the same, though the clothes be different: the tree is the same, though the leaves be different: the Church is the same, though the forms be different. At the commencement of the Christian dispensation, the kingdom of God was taken from the Jews and given to a nation bringing forth the fruit thereof (Matt. xxi. 43). Some of the Jewish branches were then broken off, and a wild Gentile olive-tree was grafted in, and thus made to partake of the root and fatness of the olive-tree (Rom. xi. 17). The Gentile sheep were brought into the fold, where the Jewish believers already were (John x. 16). Christ, our peace, made Jew and Gentile one, and broke down the middle wall of partition between them (Eph. ii. 14). But, through all these changes, the Church, in all its essential parts, remained unchanged: it was the same kingdom that was taken from the Jew that was given to the Gentiles: it was the same olive-tree from which the Jewish branches were broken off that had the Gentiles grafted in: it was the same fold, only with other of Christ's sheep brought into it: it was the same chamber, only enlarged by the removal of a partition wall. *The Church, therefore, into whose membership infants were at the beginning introduced, is essentially the same Church that exists in the world still.*

4. The Church membership of infants has never been set aside. It was, as we have seen, the original appointment of God himself. It existed 430 years before the law of Moses was given. It was the established practice of the Church of God for two thousand years. Something very clear and explicit is required to nullify an appointment of God, so universally observed and so long established. Among the changes of the new economy, has the Church membership of infants been annulled and set aside? We search, with anxiety, the inspired records of the New Testament Church, to know whether children are to be excluded, while their believing parents are taken in—whether infants occupy a worse ecclesiastical position now than they did under the Old Dispensation. Believers are to be taken in, but there is no direction that we can find to shut their children out. We ask the Lord Jesus for guidance on this matter, and He says, "Suffer the little children to come unto me, and forbid them not" (Mark x. 14) we question Paul on this subject, and he tells us that even where one parent is a believer, the "children are holy" (I Cor. vii. 14): we seek instruction from John, and we find him writing unto little children, as members of the Christian Church (I John ii. 13). We can find, then, no authority in the New Testament for believing that the ancient practice of admitting children to membership in the Church of God has ever been set aside. Not only so, but no Anabaptist has ever yet appeared who could lay his finger on any passage of God's word, where, by command, example, or fair inference, the great principle of infant Church membership was ever reversed. A law never repealed, is, of course, always in force. We

conclude, therefore, that *the membership of infants is, at this moment, the standing law of the Church of God*. A Divine law cannot be set aside by anything short of Divine authority, and Divine authority for depriving the children of a right which they enjoyed for two thousand years, is something that, up to the present time, has never yet been brought forward.

To produce from the New Testament any express statute re-affirming the membership of infants in the Church, is what we are not bound to do. Except the Old Testament is a dead letter—"a bundle of waste paper—there is no need for it. We have shown the Divine law that established the right of infants to Church membership. The Anabaptists say, that at Christ's coming, this was abrogated. Let them show it if they can. "We insist that they shall produce Scriptural proof of God's having annulled the constitution under which we assert our right. Till they do this, our cause is invincible. He once granted to His Church the right for which we contend; and nothing but His own act can take it away. We want to see the act of abrogation; we must see it in the New Testament; for there it is; if it is at all. Point it out, and we have done. Till then, we shall rejoice in the consolation of calling upon God as our God, and the God of our seed."[4] Or, to use the words of a writer of their own, "A Divine law must continue obligatory until it is repealed by Divine authority." Now, let the Anabaptist produce the authority by which the Divine law of infant Church membership is repealed. But this he knows he can never do.

5. Infants being thus entitled by the Divine law to Church membership, the only question that remains, is as to the way in which that membership is to be acknowledged—is it to be with baptism or without it? To receive them as members *without* baptism, is to say, in other words, that baptism is useless, and to strike at its very existence as an ordinance in the Church of God: to receive them *with* baptism, is to say that infants are to be baptized. This is strengthened by the consideration that the children of God's people are recognised, under the Old Dispensation, as members of the Church, by the same ordinance as their parents; it was the same rite that was administered to the old man of a hundred years, and to the infant only eight days old. In the absence of any intimation to the reverse, we conclude that the children of God's people are to be received to membership, under the New Dispensation,

---

[4] *Essays on the Church of God.* No. V. By J. M. Mason, D. D.

by the same ordinance as their parents are. Now, we find by the Scriptures, that believing adults are to be received by baptism: the infants of believers, we conclude, are to be received by baptism also; because it has been the law from the beginning, that the ordinance which admits the parent, also admits the child. We cannot resist the conclusion that *it is the appointment of God that the infants of believers are to be admitted to Church membership by Baptism.*

Infant baptism, being thus the appointment of God, to attend to it is a duty—to neglect it is a sin. The believer who objects to have his children baptized, is quarrelling with a Divine ordinance, omitting to claim the spiritual promises and privileges of God's covenant, practically renouncing, in the name of his children, all interest in that covenant. It is a piece of greater cruelty and folly than was perpetrated by Esau; Esau parted with his own birthright, but the man who repudiates infant baptism, parts with his children's; Esau sold his birthright for something, but this man deliberately flings away a privilege, and receives nothing in return. Thus, the Anabaptist despises his children's birthright.

IV. The Apostolic Commission.

The commission given by Christ to the Apostles after the resurrection, is sometimes confidently quoted as if it nullified the argument which we have now advanced. That commission is in these words—"Go ye, therefore, and teach all nations, baptizing them in the name of the Father, and of the Son, and of the Holy Ghost; teaching them to observe all things whatsoever I have commanded" (Matt. xxviii. 19,20). Here we see, *first*, the *parties* among whom the Apostles were to labour, "all nations"—not the Jews only, but the Gentiles: *second*, the *work* to be done—"*teach,*" or, as it is more correctly translated, "disciple" all nations: *third*, the *means* by which the work of discipling was to be done—baptizing them and teaching them. But how this proves that the children of believers are not to be baptized, it is very difficult to discover. If to "make disciples of all nations" meant to make disciples of adults only, and if infants were wholly incapable of baptism and instruction, the commission, it is clear, would not contemplate their case: but, if we find elsewhere that the infants of God's people are entitled to the privilege of Church membership, the commission must be understood in accordance therewith. The Word of God cannot contradict itself. Narrow it down to authorize merely the baptism of believing adults—an interpretation of which it is scarcely capable—still a command to baptize believing adults does not necessarily exclude infants, and that infants are entitled to Church membership we learn from other passages of the Word of God.

For the intelligent reader it would not be necessary to notice the argument that because the word *teach*, or *make disciples* of, occurs in the passage *before* the word *baptizing*, that, therefore, in each case it is necessary to *disciple* the individual before he is baptized. But, with the ignorant, this is considered an irresistible argument, and, on this account, it is well to notice it. Now, it is quite true, that if an apostle, or any other missionary, go forth to evangelize a heathen nation, he must teach the truth before he can find any to believe it, and he must, of course, have believers before it is possible for him to baptize the children of believers. So that if the Apostles were commanded to make disciples before they baptized, this would be no difficulty in the way of the baptism of infants; the missionary has always to teach before he baptizes—he has to convert the parent before he can baptize the child. But any man who chooses to examine, may see that this is not necessarily taught in the passage. When the Lord commands the Apostles to *make disciples of all nations*, he shows them, in general, *the work* that they are to do: when he adds, *baptizing* and *teaching* them, He specifies in detail the way in which the work of making disciples is to be done—"baptizing them in the name of the Father, and the Son, and of the Holy Ghost; teaching them to observe all things whatsoever I have commanded." This is an unfortunate passage for our Anabaptist friends: henceforth it should cease to be a favourite with them, for the way of discipling all nations prescribed in the commission, even interpreted in their own way, is to baptize first and instruct afterwards.

There would be some plausibility in the Anabaptist interpretation, if the commission read "make disciples of all nations *and* baptize them:" but it is a very different form of expression to say, "make disciples of all nations, baptizing and teaching." One parallel to it is found in I Tim. ii. 8—"I will, therefore, that men pray everywhere, lifting up holy hands without wrath and doubting." Here the Apostle first states the duty—*prayer;* and then the way in which the duty is to be done—*lifting up holy hands;* but if this verse were explained as our friends would have us to do the apostolic commission, we would say that Paul's meaning is, that men are to pray first, and to lift up holy hands afterwards. A gentleman, let us say, has two men-servants, a Presbyterian and an Anabaptist, and he says to them some fine morning, "Go and coat the avenue with gravel, drawing it from the river, and spreading it on the path." After the master has retired within, the two men stand outside debating the meaning of his orders. "I think," says the Presbyterian, "that the master's meaning is plain; the work which he wishes us to do is to gravel the avenue, and the way in which we are to do it is to draw the gravel from the river, and spread it on the path." "Not at all," says the other, "that is more of your Presbyterian nonsense. Did you not observe that the master spoke of coating the avenue before he spoke of drawing the gravel from the river? What he wants us to do is, first to put a coating of gravel on the path, and then to draw it from the river afterwards: and mark you, my good friend, I have my minister's authority for this, because this is exactly the way in which he interprets the commission that was given to the Apostles of the Lord."

An Anabaptist writer, commenting on the commission, indulges in a military illustration. He supposes Government to order the colonel of a regiment to fill up a certain company with men six feet high; the recruiting sergeants, in compliance with the orders, go forth in search of men, but the recruits, when they are measured, turn out to be five feet eight instead of six feet. He thinks, very properly, that this would be unsoldierly conduct, inasmuch as "the instructions that mentioned six feet high as the standard, forbid all under that measure to be enlisted." In like manner, he thinks that a command to baptize believers necessarily excludes infants from baptism.[5]

But this author must take his readers to be very innocent, if he expects them to regard such an illustration as a fair representation of the case. It utterly fails to exhibit our argument—nay, it does not attempt to do it. We venture to give an illustration to supply his lack of service, and then we will comment upon it, *almost in his own words*. Let us suppose that in one of the Queen's regiments it has been the practice, for very many years, to enlist full-grown men of six feet high, and also lads of ten years of age, that from their childhood they may be trained in the art of war; and suppose an order came down from the War-Office which alters the form of enlisting, and, without mentioning boys,

---

[5] *Carson on Baptism*, p. 172.

directs that, in future, all men enlisted into that regiment need only be five feet eight inches. Suppose, farther, that the recruiting sergeants would interpret the instructions in this way, that because the recruits in future may be only five feet eight, and the order does not mention boys, therefore, no more boys are to be enlisted into the regiment; and suppose they act on this principle, and that, when they return from their recruiting tour, they have no lads with them, and that, in consequence of such conduct, her Majesty's service is, for a length of time, deprived of the service of those who can be trained as men of war from their youth. The colonel is in high displeasure, and calls the sergeants to account for their unsoldierly conduct, when out steps one of the most flippant of them all, instructed by Dr. Carson, who stands forward in his defence—"Stop a little, Colonel, I will prove to you that our conduct was perfectly right. You know that in this gallant regiment the practice did long exist of enlisting men of six feet high, and boys of ten years of age; now, when the recent orders came from the War-Office, changing the mode of enlistment, and lowering the standard of the men from six feet to five feet eight, these orders never spoke of boys at all; I thought, therefore, that boys were not to be admitted into the regiment any more. Nay, more, I can assure you, good Colonel, we have the sanction of the Anabaptist Churches for this way of reasoning, though they profess the strictest adherence to the Scriptures. Dr. Carson explains his Lord's commission to baptize in the very way in which we have explained our commission to enlist. If he treats the commission of the Lord of heaven in that way, it surely cannot be blameable in us to treat your commission in a similar way. We thought that, when the men in the regiment might, in future, be five feet eight, that lads, as formerly, would not be required." "You thought, sir," says the Colonel, "you reasoned! Who authorised you to reason on the subject? Your business was to obey. Your orders were so plain that they could not be mistaken. You knew it was always the peculiar practice of this regiment, from the first day of its existence, to enlist lads as well as men into the Queen's service. You knew that recent orders lowered the standard height of the men only, and did not interfere with the established practice in regard to boys. You had no right to reason, then, that the order spoke of boys, when it only spoke of men. Your conduct is unsoldierly, and would subvert all discipline. Drop your swords, take up your muskets, and return to the ranks." And does the Anabaptist expect a "well done, good and faithful servant," for conduct that would disgrace a recruiting sergeant? If Paul had ever seen such a man, and heard him reason, he might not have addressed him altogether in the style wherein he spoke to Elymas the sorcerer, but he certainly would have said—*Wilt thou not cease to pervert the right ways of the Lord?*

V. Additional Considerations.

The argument by which we prove the right of children to baptism is strictly analogous to that by which we prove the perpetual obligation of the Lord's Day. The Anabaptist is compelled on that subject to adopt the same line of argument that we do on baptism. He goes back to the Old Testament Dispensation to find there the principle of one day's rest after six days' work, in the same way as we go back to find the principle of the church membership of infants. He finds that the principle of resting one day out of seven existed long before the law of Moses, though it was incorporated therein; just as we find the principle of infant church membership existing from the days of Abraham, though it was incorporated in the law given at Sinai 430 years after Abraham (Gal. iii. 17). He finds that the law of the Sabbath was acknowledged by God's people down till the coming of Christ; and we find that the law of the church membership of infants was acknowledged by them down till the same period. Finding nothing in the New Testament to set aside the principle of one day's rest after six days' work, he considers that the law of the Sabbath is still in force; exactly as we, finding nothing in the New Testament to set aside the principle of infant church membership, conclude that that portion of the Divine law is in full force still. He discovers, however, that the New Testament introduces a modification, in consequence of which he considers himself warranted in devoting the first day of the week instead of the last to purposes of rest and worship: and we discover, too, that the New Testament introduces a modification, in consequence of which we consider ourselves warranted in recognising the church membership of infants by the ordinance of baptism, instead of by the ordinance of circumcision. He maintains that the change from the seventh to the first day of the week does not interfere with the great unrepealed principle of one day's rest after six days' work, and he concludes, therefore, that the law of the Sabbath is a perpetual ordinance: and we maintain that the change of the initiatory rite from circumcision to baptism does not interfere with the great unrepealed principle of infant membership; and we conclude, therefore, that infant membership in the Church of God is a perpetual ordinance. He insists that if men do not discover sufficient authority in the New Testament for the change of day, this does not free them from the law of the Sabbath, but binds them to keep it on the seventh day instead of the first: and we insist that if men do not see sufficient authority in the New Testament for infant baptism, this does not free them from the law of infant church membership, but binds them to acknowledge that membership by circumcising instead of baptizing them. In short, the mode of proof is the same exactly in the one case as it is in the other. So much is this the case, that that section of Anabaptists known as Plymouth Brethren, with admirable consistency, deny the perpetual obligation of the Sabbath as well as the church membership of infants. The ordinary Anabaptist shrinks from this; he holds by the Sabbath, and rejects infant baptism; and, strange to tell, the very same argument which, on the one subject, he thinks ought to convince everybody, he asserts, on the other subject, should convince nobody. The same proof that, in the one case, pleases him well, on the other does not please him at all. Prejudice, it is to be feared, warps the judgment of these good people even more than they themselves suspect.

The argument for infant baptism, as detailed in a previous chapter, is confirmed by various considerations, which also go to show how the practice harmonizes completely with other facts and statements of the Word of God.

1. *The love and respect the Lord Jesus often showed for children.* "He shall feed His flock like a shepherd: He shall gather the lambs with His arm, and carry them in His bosom" (Isa. xl. II). "And Jesus called a little child unto Him, and set him in the midst of them, and said, Verily, I say unto you, Except ye be converted, and become as little children, ye shall not enter the kingdom of heaven" (Matt. xviii. 2, 3). "And He took them up in His arms, put His hands upon them, and blessed them" (Mark x. 16). "Jesus saith to Simon Peter, Simon, son of Jonas, lovest thou me more than these? He saith unto Him, Yea, Lord; thou knowest that I love thee. He saith unto him, "Feed my lambs" (John xxi. 15). These passages show. at the very least, that the Lord Jesus entertains no dislike to little children. But would it not be fair to conclude that He cherished no fondness for them, if, without assigning a

reason, He has deprived them of a precious privilege that once was theirs, and excluded them from His Church? The Good Shepherd carries the lambs in His bosom, but the Anabaptist would have us believe that He takes the sheep into the fold and shuts out the lambs.

2. *To receive a little child in Christ's name is a duty which Christ Himself recommends.* "And Jesus took a child, and set him in the midst of them: and when He had taken him in His arms, He said unto them, Whosoever shall receive one of such children in my name, receiveth me" (Mark ix. 36, 37). To receive any one, is to treat him as becomes the station and position that he fills. Christ came to His own, and His own received Him not (John i. 11), that is, did not treat Him with the respect due to His rank and dignity. The expression, "in my name," is explained (Mark ix. 41) to mean "because ye belong to Christ." To receive a little child in Christ's name is to treat it as belonging to Christ. But which Church treats little children as belonging to Christ—the Church that receives them to its bosom, or the Church that excludes them, as being unfit for membership?

3. *There is a distinction made between the children of believers and those of unbelievers.* "The unbelieving husband is sanctified by the wife, and the unbelieving wife is sanctified by the husband: else were your children unclean; but now are they holy" (I Cor. vii. 14). Whatever be the meaning attached to the terms here used, they make a distinction between the children of the believer and those of the unbeliever; even where one parent is a believer, the Apostle tells us the children are holy, otherwise they would be unclean. Now, this distinction Anabaptism fails to recognise, for, by withholding baptism, it treats the children of God's saints as it treats the children of God's enemies, pronouncing both, so far as admission to the Church is concerned, to be equally unclean.

But the text teaches much more than this. The word *holiness* has two senses in Scripture, the one being purity of moral character, the other consecration to God. In the former sense, the Divine Being, the unfallen angels, and the saints, are said to be *holy*, that is, free from the impurity of sin. In the other, the Sabbath, the high priests' garments, the vessels of the tabernacle, the temple, and the land in which the Israelites lived, are said to be holy; that is, consecrated to God. In this sense the whole nation of Israel is said to be holy (Lev. xx. 26; Ezra ix. 2), because they were chosen from the other nations, and separated to the service of God. In the same sense the child of Jewish parents was reckoned holy. It was, of course, a sinner—by nature a child of wrath, as other children are—but being the child of God's people, it was counted as God's; it received in the flesh the seal of His covenant; it was thus marked as His property; it was henceforth reckoned holy, that is, devoted to God. Now, this style of speech Paul transfers from the Jewish to the Christian Church; and he teaches that if one parent only be a believer, the children are not to be counted with the world, but with the Church, not with the kingdom of Satan, but with the kingdom of Christ, not among God's enemies, but among His professing people. If, in such circumstances, the child of Jewish parents had a right to be received by the initiatory rite of the Old Dispensation, the child of Christian parents has a right to be received by the initiatory rite of the New— in other words, to be baptized. Should it live to reach that period of life when it becomes able to judge and act for itself, and of course ceases to be represented by its parents, its own conduct is from that time to determine the relation in which it is to stand to the Church of God.

The value of the passage in Corinthians is not so much that it states anything positive on the subject of baptism, as that it takes for granted the principle that the character of the parent is to determine the way in which we are to regard his child under the New as well as under the Old Dispensation. As the child of a Jew is to be treated as a Jew, so now the child of a Christian is to be treated as a Christian if one parent is a believer, the children, in virtue of their connexion with that parent, are to be reckoned holy. A believer is not his own—his body, his soul, his property, all are God's, and are consecrated to Him. But the above passage is valuable, for it shows that his children also are God's: and when the Christian parent presents his child in baptism, that is his acknowledgment of God's claim. Infant baptism furnishes the believer with a suitable opportunity of saying, in the most expressive form, that his children belong to God; but Anabaptism denies the parent such an opportunity, puts the child of a saint on a level with the child of an infidel, and refuses to recognise it as holy; that is, the possession and property of God.

The assertion that the words *holy* and *unclean* are to be understood here in the sense of *legitimate* and *illegitimate*, and that the meaning of the passage is, that the children of a believing parent are not bastards! is too absurd to be seriously considered. The word translated *holy,* though occurring, as Dr.

Wilson has shown, above seven hundred times in the Septuagint, Apocrypha, and New Testament, never means *legitimate* in any instance whatsoever. To say, therefore, that it has such a meaning, only proves the desperate expedients to which prejudice has recourse in order to evade an argument.

4. *The child of the believer is to be presented publicly to the Lord.* In Luke II. 22, 23, we read of the child Jesus being brought by his parents to present him to the Lord. The reason assigned for this is that he was *holy*—not in the sense of being free from sin, though that was true, but in the sense of being devoted to God. As a first-born son, he was the peculiar property of God, and therefore to be presented to Him; for "every male that openeth the womb shall be called holy to the Lord." Now, under the Gospel, we learn from I Cor. vii. 14, that the child of every Christian parent, whether a first-born child or not, is in the same position. "Else were your children unclean; but now are they holy." If the first-born in Israel was to be presented to God because it was holy, the children of the believer are to be presented publicly to Him for the same reason. They, too, are "holy—the property of God. Now, the baptism of a child affords the parent a suitable time for this public presentation to God. We present our children to God in their baptism. But were we Anabaptists, we would not be allowed by our system any public opportunity of doing this. Being contrary to Anabaptist principles, it is, in reality, never done by them.

5. *Christ Himself asserts the Church membership of infants* (Matt. xix. 14). "Jesus said, Suffer little children, and forbid them not, to come unto me: for of such is the kingdom of heaven." If the kingdom of heaven in this passage is understood to mean the state of glory, it only strengthens our argument; for if children may enter the Church above, they are surely fit to enter the Church below; the greater privilege includes the less. But the phrase is generally understood to signify the Gospel Church, and the Saviour here states, as a reason why children should be permitted to approach Him, that such as they belong to the membership of that Church. Since, therefore, children form a portion of the membership of the Church, they are entitled to the rights of membership, and one of these rights is baptism.

Attempts have been made to weaken the force of this argument, by the allegation that the passage means that children are to come to Christ because that adults, who resemble children in character, belong to the membership of this Church. This exposition is open, however, to two very grave objections.

First, it puts a sentiment akin to nonsense into the lips of Him from whom no folly ever fell. How absurd for the Lord Jesus to give, as a reason for bringing children to Him, that men, teachable and humble as children, belong to His Church. The same reason would have served equally well for bringing doves to Christ for His blessing; for the irrational creatures are capable of receiving the Divine blessing (Gen. i. 22), and Christ's disciples are to be harmless as doves. Imagine Christ to say, Suffer these *doves* to come unto me, for of such is the kingdom of heaven! Yet that sentiment is exactly parallel to that which the Anabaptist exposition attributes to Him in whom all the treasures of wisdom are hid. *Second*, this interpretation assigns to the word *such* a meaning that it never has, as if it denoted the resemblance that exists between objects of a different class, whereas it denotes the resemblance that exists between objects of the same class. It never denotes the resemblance that exists, for instance, between a man and a child, but that which exists between some men and other men, between some children and other children. Thus, in Acts xxii. 22, "Away with such a fellow from the earth," simply means, away with any fellow of *the same kind as this fellow* from the earth. Other examples are found in John iv. 23; Heb. vii. 26, and many other places; *such* always referring to persons or objects of *the same kind* as that immediately in hand. Interpreting the passage in question as we do others of a similar kind, we understand Christ to say that children must be allowed to come to Him, for children like those before Him belong to His Church on earth. Christ did not baptize these children, for Christian baptism was not then instituted; but when He affirms that of such is the kingdom of heaven, He informs us that children form a portion of the membership of His Church; and, this being the case, they have a right to the privileges of membership and to this, baptism is only the first step.

6. *The Apostles themselves baptized households.* The family of Lydia was baptized (Acts xvi. 15), although there is no evidence, not the slightest, to show that any of her household believed except herself. Two other cases we have, in the jailer (Acts xvi. 33) and Stephanas (I Cor. i. 16), whose households were baptized, although it is very uncertain, as every man competent to examine the Greek original of Acts xvi. 34, and I Cor. xvi. 15, knows very well, whether these households believed or not. It is remarkable, however, that of the eleven distinct cases of baptism recorded in Scripture, three of these are

family baptisms, proving that such was a common practice in apostolic times. Now, on the principle that we adopt, that the younger portion of the household are entitled to church membership in virtue of their relationship to a believing parent, these family baptisms might be expected: but on Anabaptist principles, such events must border on the miraculous. To keep these three cases from proving infant baptism, he requires the reader of Scripture to believe that there were no children in any of these three households—that every member of these three families was capable of faith— and that, at the very time the head of each house believed, all the other persons in the house believed also. Now, is this likely? On the contrary, if there was one infant in any of those three houses, infant baptism receives an additional proof. Let the reader judge which view is the most natural, the most probable, and most in accordance with the general tenor of the Word of God. The fact that it was a common practice for the Apostles to baptize households, though in itself not conclusive, is certainly a strong consideration in favour of baptizing children, since children form an important feature of most households. Attempts have been made to show that the apostolic commission would exclude the baptism of infants, even if they were found in those households. But that, as we have seen, is a mistake; the commission commands the Apostles to baptize the *nations*, in which, of course, infants are included. To use it for such a purpose, would be to make the law a comment on the practice, whereas it is the practice of the Apostles that determines the sense in which they understood the law: and to be obliged to fall back on the commission in order to exclude infants from these households, only betrays a consciousness on the part of those who adopt this expedient, that without the help of the commission they cannot themselves resist the belief that the baptism of households involves the baptism of infants.

7. *Children are found in the membership of Churches planted by the Apostles.* It is a well-known fact, that the Epistles of Paul were mostly all addressed to Churches—to those companies of Christians that were collected, by the preaching of the Word, out of the Gentile and Jewish population. The Epistle to the Ephesians is addressed "to the saints which are in Ephesus, and to the faithful in Christ Jesus" (Eph. i. 1); and yet it is certain that there were children in that very Church of Ephesus, for Paul addresses them specially, as a component part of the Church—"Children, obey your parents, in the Lord: for

this is right (Eph. vi. 1). The Epistle to the Colossians is addressed "to the saints and faithful brethren in Christ which are at Colosse" (Col. i. 1, 2); and in that very Epistle, children are addressed among the members of the Church—"Children, obey your parents in all things: for this is well-pleasing unto the Lord (Col, iii 20). Such passages show clearly that children were in the Churches that were planted by the Apostles. This being the case, the question naturally arises, *How did they get in?* Was it by baptism, or without it? If it was without baptism, then baptism has ceased to be the initiatory rite of the Christian Church, and has lost all its significance; if they were admitted by baptism, there remains no further question about the duty of baptizing the children of believers. Any man, whose prejudices do not blind him utterly, must see that the Churches planted by the Apostles were not constituted on the Anabaptist plan. The apostolic Churches had children in them, for the Apostles, in writing to the Churches, addressed themselves to children. The Anabaptist Churches have no children in their membership, but plume themselves on the circumstance that they keep children out: therefore, it is clear the Anabaptist Churches are not apostolic Churches.[6]

Every man must see how very much these considerations go to corroborate the main argument for infant baptism. The right of the children of believers to church membership underlies the statements that meet us so often in the New Testament Scriptures, and the admission of this fact casts light on passages that otherwise would be dark and difficult. In that fact we have evidence of how the Good Shepherd loves the young, and gathers them into the fold; but the Anabaptist would have us believe that the Good Shepherd admits the sheep, and shuts out the lambs. When we baptize an infant, we receive a little child in Christ's name; but, although that is a duty recommended in the Scriptures (Mark ix. 37), the Anabaptist laughs it to scorn. We distinguish between the children of believers and the children of unbelievers, by baptizing the holy, and refusing baptism to the unclean; but Anabaptism makes no such distinction, for it treats as unclean those to whom the Spirit of God bears witness that they are holy, and will not allow them to

---

[6] So keenly is the force of this argument felt. that some Anabaptist Churches. we understand, are now admitting to membership young persons at a very early age. Some are taken in so early as thirteen, and some at nine. This is a move in the right direction. There will soon be but a year or two between us.

be publicly presented to the Lord. Christ, Himself, asserts of children that "of such is the kingdom of heaven," and we, by baptism, recognise them as such: but Anabaptism refuses to acknowledge them, and attempts to explain away the law of the kingdom by which their membership is secured. It was a common practice of the Apostles to baptize households: but, except to lame one of our arguments, the baptism of a whole family at the same time would not be heard of in the history of an Anabaptist mission twice in a generation. Children were in the apostolic Churches: but to admit a child under nine years of age would be reckoned, by an Anabaptist Church, heresy and pollution. Let the candid reader decide for himself which system, theirs or ours, is most accordant with the letter and spirit of the Word of God.

VI. No proof on the Anabaptist side.

We have now done with our direct statement. The weightiest objections advanced against the practice of administering baptism to the children of believers have been examined and found wanting. Like the ghosts of which we read in fable, they look formidable and frightful at a distance, but they vanish as we draw near. We have stated candidly the evidence that induces us to recognise by baptism the church membership of infants, and that evidence has been strengthened by various considerations drawn from the Word of God. We have kept nothing back, but, so far as our space permits, we have stated, for the satisfaction of the reader, the reasons that induce us to admit by baptism the infant children of believers.

Now, let the Anabaptists be equally honest and explicit. Their plan of treating the children of believers is to keep them unbaptized till they reach such a mature age as is necessary to enable them to understand the Gospel, and profess faith for themselves. This is their plan. Let them state the evidence from the Word of God that warrants them to act in this way. We have plainly stated the evidence for our practice: let them state the evidence for theirs. Let them state one text that bids them to keep the child of a believer unbaptized. *Let them produce one solitary example from the Scriptures, of one who was the child of Christian parents at his birth, but who did not receive baptism till he made a personal profession of his faith.* If the Scripture be so much on their side as they pretend, they should have no difficulty here. The New Testament history, from Pentecost till the death of the Apostle John, covers the space of sixty or seventy years, surely time enough to allow the infants of many believing Christian parents to grow up to manhood, and to enter the Church on their own profession of faith. Let them produce one such case from Scripture if they can. I am willing to rest the whole question on this issue. Let them name the case in Scripture of the child of Christian parents who was treated on their plan and not on ours. Let them show me one clear case of this, and I will never again pour water on an infant. But there is no fear that they will ever try.

VII. The Parable of the City Park.

About 500 years ago there was a rich and princely nobleman, whose castle stood in the neighbourhood of a great city. The mayor of the city and this nobleman were on such intimate terms, that even in those days of feudal power the baron was not ashamed to acknowledge the honest burgher as his friend. The nobleman having determined to remove his family to a foreign country, was sad at the prospect of parting with the mayor, and he generously promised to bestow on him, and the city which he represented, some munificent gift that would prove to other ages a lasting memorial of their friendship. There was a beautiful garden in the precincts of the city, planted with all manner of rare plants, and flowers, and fruit trees, which had for generations been the property of the baron's ancestors; and it occurred to him that to allow the mayor and aldermen of the city the use of this garden, in the absence of his own family, would be counted by the corporation a strong expression of personal goodwill. Accordingly, he gave directions that the mayor and aldermen, together with their children, should have a right of entrance to the garden, and that the same privilege should be enjoyed by their successors.

After the baron's departure the aldermen entered on possession of the garden, and enjoyed it very much. They were grateful for the honour, and took advantage of the privilege it brought within their reach. It was a pleasant sight—one that their less fortunate fellow-citizens often envied—to see those portly burghers, after a hard day's business in the city, enjoying themselves in that delicious retreat. The parents might be seen sitting in the shade, the children romping on the grass—one climbing the fruit tree to rob it of its clusters, another sailing his paper boat upon the lake, another culling flowers for a nosegay, another—the youngest of all—crowing in the nurse's arms. In this way the aldermen of the city and their children enjoyed that princely pleasure-ground for 250 years.

About the end of that time, the lord of the soil, the lineal descendant of the original donor, himself the scion of a race of nobles, visited the inheritance of his fathers. He found that the state of affairs was very different from what he knew it had been 250 years before. The good mayor and all that generation were many years dead; the city had grown more populous and wealthy. The garden, indeed, was as beautiful as ever, but the aldermen who enjoyed the privilege of entering it, had become degenerate; they had grown insolent and proud; they looked down upon the other citizens as the very dregs of the earth; they had lost that love and attachment to the lord of the soil by which their predecessors had been distinguished 250 years before, and they could no longer be counted among the nobleman's friends. Indeed, they wore the mask of friendship, but they were enemies at heart.

The young baron, having made many fruitless efforts to reform these wicked men, resolved to deprive them of their privilege, and bestow it on others who would prove themselves more worthy. He enlarged the garden, by throwing into it a neighbouring common, and spared no expense in making it more beautiful than ever. It was made so large as to be a park rather than a garden. The gate, that in old times was so strait that it scarcely would admit a rotund alderman, was now so much widened that a coach and six could drive through it with ease. A new staff of servants was appointed to keep the grounds in order, and to watch the gate, each in his turn; and instructions were given to the gatekeepers in these words—EVERY FRIEND OF MINE MAY ENTER HERE, BUT NO ADMISSION FOR MY ENEMIES. This new regulation made a great change. It abolished the invidious distinction that had hitherto existed between the aldermen and other citizens; it opened the park gate to any citizen whatever, who cherished friendly feelings for the absent peer.

The very first day that the new regulation came in force, there were 3000 citizens who claimed admission as the friends of the noble owner, and who were admitted accordingly. Henceforth that beautiful park was every day crowded with visitors. The citizens, in former times, had always seen the aldermen take their children with them into these grounds, and knew that this was done by the express directions of the original donor; and, as the young baron, on his late visit, left no directions to the contrary, they always took their children with them to the park, no one forbidding them. Two hundred years more passed by, and, during all that time, it is not on record that any gatekeeper refused the right of entrance to the child of any citizen who was known to be a friend of his master.

Some fifty years ago, however, there was a gatekeeper stationed at the park gate who took a very peculiar view of his duty. He thought that the original directions to admit children were not in force now; that the arrangements made by the young baron, when he visited the city two hundred years before, had set the ancient directions aside; that all the gatekeepers who had preceded him for two centuries were acting in the face of their instructions when admitting children. For these reasons, he expressed his determination to admit them no more. This whim called forth considerable remark at the time; but as the man in the main was a good body, and professed nice scruples of conscience in the matter, few citizens gave themselves any concern about him or his crotchet more particularly as all the other gatekeepers, knowing that they served a good master, put a generous interpretation on the baron's orders, and opened their gates freely to the children of his friends. But, for the last fifty years, it has so happened that there is always one of these park-rangers who thinks it his duty to exclude children; and, although the men are often changed, there is always one of them who strives to put the narrowest constructions possible on the master's order, and when he sees a child coming, runs and locks the gate.

Not long ago, it came to pass that a citizen, distinguished for his ardent attachment to the absent nobleman, obtained a day's leisure, and agreed with his family that he and they would spend the holiday amid the fresh air and leafy bowers of the city park. The youngsters of the house were in great glee, and soon made themselves ready for the day's enjoyment, while nurse, to her great delight, got leave to come along, carrying baby in her arms. At an early hour in the forenoon, the whole household sallied forth, and that day the sunshine seemed more glorious, and everything looked more lovely than was wont, as the whole party gaily tripped along. But, 'to their dismay, when they reached the park, it was the surly porter who was in charge that day; and when the official saw the whole household approach, his conscience became doubly tender, and he grasped the key of office with a firmer grasp, and a storm gathered on his brow. A shadow fell on the faces of the children at the sight of him, for, although they could not fathom his motives, yet they knew, by instinct, that that dark man was not their friend. The citizen was no stranger to human nature; he knew that the mind of the gatekeeper was too deeply steeped in prejudice to be open to conviction, that it furnished him with an exquisite pleasure to represent himself as much more conscientious and faithful than the other gatekeepers, and that custom had now so wedded him to his oddities and whims, that life would, for him, lose half its pleasures, if he should have to renounce them. Nevertheless, he determined to try the effect of a little reasoning upon him; whereupon the following dialogue ensued between them:—

CITIZEN. Hallo! gatekeeper, open this gate.

GATEKEEPER. With pleasure, sir, to you and your good lady, for you are both known to be my master's friends; but these children cannot be admitted.

CIT. How is that? Have orders reached you lately to exclude the children?

GAT. No, sir: but the present lord is known to be of the same mind with the baron who visited us 250 years ago, and who left us the orders by which we are now guided.

CIT. Well, I have often read the instructions; they are printed in large letters over this gate: but I never could see anything in them that necessarily shuts out the children.

GAT. But you certainly must see that the words contain no command to admit them.

CIT. Granting that the order contains no command either to admit or to exclude them, that only proves that the baron did not mean to disturb the established practice in regard to children; and you know that, for 250 years before his visit, it was the practice to admit them.

GAT. I admit that the children of the aldermen were admitted, with the baron's approval, during the time you name.

CIT. So far well. I ask you now, can you show me anything that annuls the law, changes the practice, and commands you to deny to children the right of entrance?

GAT. I cannot show you a direct command; but I can show you what is as good.

CIT. Then, by all means, let us have it.

GAT. Look to that writing on the wall, and see the command there given to the porters—"*Every friend of mine may enter here, but no admission for my enemies.*" Now, sir, you know infants are too young to be capable of friendship, and that being the case, they have no right to be here. Does not this very commission exclude children?

CIT. I do not see that is does; the order under which you act confers the privilege that once was enjoyed by the aldermen on every citizen who is the baron's friend; and, as the aldermen had a right to enter and take their children with them, so any friend of your master has the right now to enter and take his children with him; and as your orders do not name children, that shows that it was not the design of the baron to strip them of a privilege which they enjoyed already. So, open the gate, and let the children pass.

GAT. Indeed I will not; infants are not capable of friendship, and, of course, cannot be admitted as friends.

CIT. True, they cannot be admitted as friends; but that only shows that the qualification necessary for their parents is not necessary for them; and when the parents are known to be the master's friends, it is only fair to regard the whole family on the same side, till its members are guilty of some act that proves their want of friendship, and then I have no objection that you deal with them accordingly.

GAT. Say as you please, I will not admit them till they prove their friendship by acts.

CIT. Take into account that the baron enlarged this park, widened this gate, and made provision for a large accession of visitors, showing himself to be kind and generous; but you interpret his instructions in such a way as to restrict his generosity; you, in opposition to the spirit of his actions, represent him as repulsive and austere, and, without express authority, you take away from a large and important class in the community a privilege that you admit yourself belonged to them for 250 years. The baron would not be guilty of doing anything so harsh without good reasons; but he has assigned no reasons, and given no orders to that effect which I am able to discover.

GAT. Sir, it is presumptuous in you to be thus guided by carnal reason: you may be sure I am right, there is no mistake about it. But permit me to ask, how am I to know that it is the will of the present baron to admit children?

CIT. From the simple fact that he has never countermanded the original orders in regard to children. Those orders hold good till they are revoked by the same authority as enacted them at first.

GAT. You need not think to change me; I will never admit children at this gate.

CIT. True; but you must have patience to hear argument on the subject. Is it not known that the present lord has inherited the sentiments of his ancestor who enlarged these grounds? And is it not on record that he was fond of children, that he sometimes took them up in his arms, and blessed them; and that, on one occasion when his ignorant servants tried to keep children away from him, he administered to his followers a sharp rebuke. Now, when you shut children out of the park, whether is your conduct more in accordance with the spirit of the baron, or with that of his narrow-minded followers?

GAT. Do you suppose that it is my business to answer questions? I have other duties to mind.

CIT. Do you not know the bar0n once said that children must be allowed to come to him, for this park was intended for such as they?

GAT. Friend, you quite mistake that saying: the true meaning is, that children should be allowed to approach him, because men, in some respects like children, have the right of entrance to his park.

CIT. Well, if that exposition can satisfy you, you yourself are one of those of whom you speak—"Men, in some respects like children."

GAT. Sir, I perceive you sit in the chair of the scorner.

CIT. Pardon me, I can scarcely help it. However, did not the baron once say, He that receiveth one of these children in my name receiveth me? If so; when you reject the children what are you doing to the master?

GAT. Very true, he did say these words; but he did not bid me to open the park gate to them.

CIT. Did not the master go so far as to make a distinction between the children of his friends and those of his enemies, calling the one class holy, and the other unclean; but you treat both as unclean when you shut all together out of the park.

GAT. Will you not understand language, notwithstanding all I can say to you? When he said that the children of his friends were holy, he only meant that they were not bastards.

CIT. Well, you are a strange interpreter! You stop at nothing to turn aside an argument.

GAT. If you do not like it, I cannot help it. I am not bound to please you with interpretations.

CIT. The gatekeepers, whom the baron appointed at his last visit to the city, must have known his lordship's pleasure better than you, who never saw his face, and they admitted whole families into these grounds. History tells us how a citizen called Lydia, and one called Stephanas, and another—I forget his name—the governor of the city jail, had their whole households admitted. Now, I only ask you to do for my family what these primitive porters did for theirs.

GAT. But you must prove to me that there was a child in those households you have named.

CIT. Your notions of logic seem as strange as your expositions. When you assert that a privilege which belonged to children for 250 years is taken from them, it is your place to prove your statement. If you fail to do this, the privilege continues as a matter of course. A privilege never lost is still ours in possession. Meanwhile, take notice how different your conduct is from that of the first gatekeepers; they admitted whole families, and you do not.

GAT. But my grandfather was a gatekeeper here, and I know it was his opinion that no children were in these households.

CIT. It would be as well for you to go by the baron's orders, and never heed your grandfather.

GAT. Now, that is where you show your ignorance, and malice, and impudence: the opinions of my grandfather and the baron's orders were always in harmony. My grandfather was a great man; he was always right on every subject and it is only pure spite and malice in you that tempts you to think otherwise.

CIT. Keep your temper, my good friend; your grandfather was, no doubt, a worthy gentleman, and I have no objection that you think him infallible if you please. But have we not good authority for saying that children were in this park in the time of the first gatekeepers; and, as they were in, I presume they must have passed through this gate.

Gat. I have given you sufficient reason for my conduct: it is not necessary that I explain every difficulty that you, and troublesome fellows like you, may suggest.

Cit. Pardon me, good sir, for saying anything that might imply that any relative of yours ever could be wrong in his opinion. But you know we have a true history that gives an account of transactions that took place here for seventy years after the new arrangements came into force; and I ask you honestly to say, is it on record that the child of any friend of the baron's was ever refused admission at the gate?

Gat. There is no such record.

Cit. Then why do you keep them out?

Gat. Ask me no more of your questions.

Cit. Was there any gatekeeper, for the first 200 years after the first appointment at the time of the baron's visit, who shut out the children?

Gat. No; but I do not see what that proves they were all wrong, of course.

Cit. Of all the gatekeepers now in office, is there one who excludes the children from the park, or understands his instructions as you do?

Gat. None. But what does that prove? Do you think I care anything for human authority?

Cit. I am sure you do not. You set no value on any human authority except your own, and, if you do not be angry, I will add your grandfather's. But I will follow you no farther at present. Argument is lost on any man with whom his own opinion stands above all argument. I will take home my children at present, and come back some other day, when I am sure to find another at the gate who knows the baron's will better than you. Were it possible for me to cherish hard thoughts of the nobleman you serve, it is the harsh, narrow-minded, bigoted conduct of the servant that would lower the master in my esteem. But far be it from me to measure that large and generous heart of his by the petty representation you give of him. There is a day coming when you will know whether your treatment of the children of his best friends meets with his approbation. Meanwhile, I leave with you a sentence from an old book that you can think of at your leisure—"It is impossible but that offences will come, but woe unto him through whom they come; it were better that a millstone was hanged about his neck, and he cast into the sea, than that he should offend one of these little ones."

The gatekeeper shrunk into his lodge as a snail into its shell, and the citizen, with his children, returned to their home. Now, the gatekeeper was an Anabaptist.

Conclusion.

The reader is now in a position to judge of the claims that Anabaptism has on the reception of Christians. It is occupied only with an ordinance, and that ordinance bearing no greater relation to the Christian system than a penny piece does to a pound sterling. Not only so, but it busies itself mainly about the mode and subjects of that ordinance. The only thing positive which it teaches is, that baptism is to be administered by putting the person into the water, instead of putting water upon the person: the other part of it is a mere negation—namely, that baptism is not to be administered to the infant children of believers. It is on husks like these that its followers are fed. Even if these principles were true, men that love the Lord should pause, and think whether such things are sufficient to justify them in putting one rent more in the Church of the living God, and in maintaining one sect more in a world that has good reason to be sick of sects. The Word of God refuses to sustain the claims of dipping; for, when Christ baptized with the Holy Ghost, He did so by making the Spirit come, fall, and rest upon the person baptized; and when we make the water of the ordinance come, fall, and rest upon the person, we baptize after Christ's example. When Anabaptism refuses to recognize, by baptism, the church membership of infants, it sets itself in opposition to an unrepealed principle of God's Word, to the established practice of two thousand years, to clear statements of the New Testament Scriptures, and to the practice of eighteen Christian centuries; while, at the same time, it can produce no case from the Scripture where the child of Christian parents was treated as they say all children should be treated. Thus it is that Anabaptism comes, with two errors in its hand, to tempt us from the way of truth.

The unpleasant effect that the sight of deformity produces on the mind is very well known. If a painter were to put upon his canvas the figure of a man, and exhibit some feature of his face in enormous disproportion to any of the others, this one defect would mar the beauty of the painting; and no matter how true it might be to nature in other respects, this alone would destroy the harmony of all. The eye of the spectator would rest upon the deformed feature, and pass over all the other parts of the picture. If the spectator were a mere boor, he might be disposed to admire the genius of the man who produced the caricature; but if he were a man of taste and judgment, a glimpse of that unsightly feature would fill him with disgust. Now, Christianity, as it is in the Old and New Testaments, is the figure that sits to have its likeness taken. Every sect undertakes to give a more correct representation of it to the world than any sister sect. But if, instead of exhibiting the Christian religion in all its relative proportions, and thus leading men to see every doctrine, and practice, and principle of the system in its proper place, whether primary or subordinate, any sect shall adopt some subordinate principle, and put it into the foreground, and make it so important that it overshadows truths vastly more important than itself, it presents to the world a distorted and deformed Christianity. Now this is what Anabaptism does. It takes up baptism and talks about it, till at last men busy themselves about the ordinance more than they do about the great truths which baptism is hiding from their view. It enlarges on the sin of infant baptism, till men at last bring themselves to believe that falsehood, and drunkenness, and dishonesty are small as compared with it. It talks about clipping, till people come at last to think that dipping is religion. Meet an Anabaptist in society, and among the first things you notice in his Christianity are his notions about dipping, and his prejudices against infants, just as in the picture the first thing that takes your attention is the one feature out of all proportion with the others. Deformity can never hide itself; and in a deformed system it is the uncomely part that always shows.

The injurious effects that connexion with a narrow-minded sect tends to produce upon the individual, find, unfortunately, too many illustrations in the world. A mind that, perhaps, originally was susceptible of cultivation and development, allows itself to be occupied so much about rites, and forms, and petty little things, that, at last, it becomes like the thoughts which harbour in it, little and petty. The better feelings of his heart, that should rise upwards to things above, and that should flow forth to all on earth who bear the image of the Heavenly, become narrowed in their flow, and gradually centre around and fix upon them, only, who cherish a crotchet similar to his own. The conduct that we expect to find in one who lays claim to a purer religion than his fellow, turns out to be no better than what is exemplified by many others who make smaller professions. And after being subject to such an influence for a series of years, a man, who once gave promise of becoming a genial and generous Christian, sinks down into a mere fault-finder—a theological cynic, whose mind is soured against every sect except his own—snarling at everything, and pleased with nothing. Such must be the effects produced on the individual, by connexion, for any length of time, with a denomination which presents any feature of Christianity in an exaggerated form to the world. It is a more serious misfortune than most men know, to belong to a sect which ever wrangles about rites and forms, and delights to split theological hairs. To be in its membership is to imbibe its spirit, and to breathe its unwholesome air. Union with some grand old church, true to the doctrines of salvation, aiming to present the world with the truth in due proportion, and frowning upon follies of every kind, is far more favourable to the growth and development of the spiritual life. The giddy and deluded may leave it to seek elsewhere a religion more congenial to their tastes: but good men will rest in its shadow, and there gather food for their souls, until the world has an end.

www.ingramcontent.com/pod-product-compliance
Lightning Source LLC
Chambersburg PA
CBHW020431010526
44118CB00010B/529